THE
WHY
FILES

Is tHeRe ReaLLy LiFe afTeR DeatH?

QuEsTioNs

about School Shootings,

Grief,

and Coming Back

as a Gerbil

JAMES N. WATKINS

CPH
SAINT LOUIS

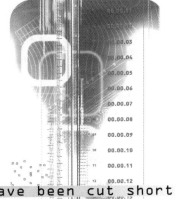

To students whose lives have been cut short
and their friends
who are left to deal with the loss

00.00.01
00.00.02
00.00.03
00.00.04
00.00.05
00.00.06
00.00.07
00.00.08
00.00.09
00.00.10
00.00.11
00.00.12
00.00.14
00.00.16
00.00.18
00.00.19
00.00.20
00.00.21
00.00.22
00.00.23
00.00.24
00.00.25
00.00.26

01 01 01 01 01 01 01 01 01 01 01 01 01 0
01 01 0101 01 01 01 01 01 0101 01 01
01 01 01 01 01 01 01 0101 01

The Why Files

When Can I Start Dating?
Questions about Love, Sex, and a Cure for Zits

Is There Really Life after Death?
Questions about School Shootings, Grief, and
Coming Back as a Gerbil

Are There Really Ghosts?
Questions about Angels, the Supernatural, and
the Psychic Friends Network

Unless otherwise indicated, Scripture quotations are taken from the Holy Bible, New International Version®. NIV®. Copyright © 1973, 1978, 1984 by International Bible Society. Used by permission of Zondervan Publishing House. All rights reserved.

Scripture quotations marked TLB are from The Living Bible copyright © 1971 by Tyndale House Publishers, Wheaton, Illinois. All rights reserved.

Scripture quotations marked KJV are from the King James or Authorized Version of the Bible.

Scripture quotations marked NRSV are taken from the New Revised Standard Version Bible, copyright © 1989, Division of Christian Education of the National Council of the Churches of Christ in the United States of America. Used by permission. All rights reserved.

Parts of this book are adapted from *Death and Beyond* copyright © 1993 by James N. Watkins, published by Tyndale House Publishers.
Some of the material about depression, suicide, and nutrition also appears in book one of this series, *When Can I Start Dating?* ©2000 by James N. Watkins.

Copyright © 1993, 2001 James N. Watkins
Published by Concordia Publishing House
3558 S. Jefferson Avenue, St. Louis, MO 63118-3968
Manufactured in the United States of America

Library of Congress Cataloging-in-Publication Data
Watkins, James, 1952-
    Is there really life after death? : questions about school shootings, grief,
and coming back as a gerbil / James N. Watkins.
        p. cm -- (The why files)
    Includes bibliographical references.
    ISBN 0-570-05247-5
1. Death--Religious aspects--Christianity. 2. Christian teenagers--Conduct of life. 3. Christian teenagers--Religious life. I. Title. II. Series.
BT825 .W318 2000
    236' .1--dc21   00-012226

1 2 3 4 5 6 7 8 9 10   10 09 08 07 06 05 04 03 02 01

CONTENTS

Foreword

I did not know Jim Watkins when I read the first edition of this book; however, I had it as a reference source for some of my earlier novels about teens facing their own mortality. When we did meet, I discovered a warm, often amusing man with a heart for teenagers and their very real problems. I liked that about him. Jim never trivializes his subjects or their concerns. He addresses them as equals.

And in a world where kids are shot down in classrooms by the very kids they know, I can't think of a better reason for *Is There Really Life after Death?* to exist. It fields questions from real kids and answers these questions in realistic and compassionate ways that reflect a biblical mind-set. Yet the book is not morbid. It's realistic and infused with wit and humor. It shoots straight, gives teens vital information, and allows them to feel that their questions (even the unasked ones!) are valid.

I can't imagine why any teen—or church youth group, for that matter—wouldn't find this book fascinating, as well as a springboard for profound discussions about life, death, and the afterlife. Many sources in our culture fill the teen mind with half-truths and untruths. I believe *Is There Really Life after Death?* can set these minds on the road of right thinking about life and eternity. And about a God who loves.

Lurlene McDaniel

Acknowledgments

Thanks to 1,000 teens from northern Indiana for their honest questions about death. Thanks to the many people who shared answers, not only from their heads but from their hearts, on the subject of death: intensive care nurses Tina Bowen and Charlene Baungartner, Mike Carlton, school counselor Marge Kavanaugh, police officer Jerry Custer, Charlie and Judy Davis, Anne Root, family practice physician Ron Sloan, funeral directors Jim and Mike Stone, and the incredible counselor I share my life with, Lois Watkins.

Thanks to my daughter, Faith, and her good friend, Jenny Grubaugh, for their invaluable input as critics of the rough draft.

And thanks to Rachel Hoyer of Concordia Publishing House for her encouragement and editorial skills. You made me look good!

Introduction to The Why Files

Jim: Excuse me. I'm taking a survey. Could you answer a few questions?

Jim: Sure, that sounds kind of interesting ... wait a minute! You can't interview me—I'm you ... I mean, you're me!

Jim: Look, Jim, I'm just doing my job.

Jim: You can't interview you, I'm me, I mean, you're me ...

Jim: Just look in the mirror and answer my first question: What do you think is the number one issue on the minds of young people today?

Jim: This is ridiculous!

Jim: Just answer the question.

Jim: Okay, fine. I just finished surveying more than 1,000 junior and senior high students on three subjects: adolescence, death, and the supernatural. I distributed the surveys in public and private schools, in rural as well as urban ...

Jim: Okay, okay, so you surveyed a bunch of people. Just answer the question: What is the number one issue on the minds of young people today?

Jim: Dating issues were the most asked questions on the adolescence survey, "Is there really life after death?" topped the death survey, and questions about God and ghosts topped our supernatural survey.

Jim: So how did you pick these three topics?

Jim: While I was editor of a teen magazine, I kept looking for articles on love and sexuality, but I never found any that honestly dealt with the issues, so I started writing them myself. Those articles eventually turned into three books on sex—everything from abortion to zits!

Then my book editor asked me to write about death, which, surprisingly, our surveys showed was of even more interest to young people than sex! So I've covered everything from grief to out-of-body experiences.

Finally, after you've spent 10 years writing about sex and death, the only bigger subject is the universe itself: God and the whole supernatural realm of angels, demons, ghosts, psychic powers, etc., etc.

Jim: And what makes you think you have the answers to all those questions?

Jim: *Well, I've worked as an author and youth speaker all my professional life, and I lived in a girls' dorm for six years, and ...*

Jim: You lived in a girls' dorm?!

Jim: *I knew interviewing myself was a bad idea!*

Jim: So?

Jim: *My wife was resident director at Indiana Wesleyan University while I worked with students on campus. What I was trying to say is that I've learned as much working with teens and young people as they've ever learned from me. And one of the most important lessons I've learned is that simple answers to complex questions don't satisfy young people.*

Jim: So you don't have a lot of answers?

Jim: *Well, I've tried to take young people and their questions seriously, plus I've done an awful lot of research to find the answers.*

Jim: So you *do* have all the answers?

Jim: *No! I don't have all the answers, but I try to share some thoughts that will help young people think about these three big subjects. I realize that each person is different, so it's hard to give an answer that satisfies everyone. That's why I try to give a general answer when young people write or e-mail questions. But I usually close with something like this:*

> *I'm glad my writing has helped you deal with some of these issues, but paper and ink are not enough. I wish*

I could sit down and talk with you face-to-face over a Diet Pepsi. Books, articles, letters, and websites can be helpful, but those can't address your one-of-a-kind situation.

You need a real, live, flesh-and-blood person to give you emotional, social, and spiritual support as well as guidance to make the right choices. I'd encourage you to talk to an adult you trust, such as a member of the clergy, a school counselor, or a youth worker.

Jim: So if your readers want to get in touch with you, how do they do that?

Jim: I love to hear from readers! They can write me c/o Concordia Publishing House, Book Development Department, 3558 South Jefferson Avenue, St. Louis, MO 63118-3968 or e-mail me at whyfiles@jameswatkins.com.

We've also set up a website with links to the resources mentioned in this book series. There are additional resources and up-to-the-minute information on sex, death, and the supernatural at www.jameswatkins.com.

Jim: Anything else in closing?

Jim: I'd like to thank each reader for buying this book. I hope the time we spend together through these pages will be not only informative, but encouraging as well. And, of course, I'd love them to tell all their friends about these three books. Or, better yet, buy a copy of all three books for all of their friends!

Jim: Well, thanks for your time. I'll let you get back to your writing.

Jim: You're welcome … I think.

Introduction

I have in my right hand, direct from my home office, today's Top Ten list: What are the top 10 questions teens ask about death?

10. What is hell like?

9. Are there such things as ghosts?

8. What is heaven like?

7. Are you able to come back as a ghost and haunt people?

6. Where do you go when you die?

5. What is death like?

4. Does death hurt?

3. Why do people have to die?

2. Do you come back as someone or something else?

And the number one response when we asked nearly 1,000 junior and senior high students, "What's a question you have about death or the possibility of life after death?"

1. Is there really life after death?

One hundred students asked the number one question. Several, however, responded with "I don't want to think about it."

You've obviously been thinking about it or you would have spent your hard-earned money on a CD rather than on this book. The recent shootings at schools across the country, as well as the increasing number of teen deaths because of automobile accidents, suicides, and AIDS, have made us all stop and think about death.

A 1980 study found that students today are "more preoccupied with thoughts of death" than young people 50 years ago. In fact, when *Psychology Today* ran a questionnaire about sex, the magazine received 10,000 responses. But a survey about death drew three times that many responses!

We're confronted with the front-page tragedies such as school shootings throughout the country. But we're also exposed to the less-sensational—but equally tragic—deaths nearer to home. For instance, while I wrote this book, two junior high and three senior high school students were killed in car accidents in our sparsely populated county.

While editor of my high school's paper, I wrote an obituary for every issue during the first semester. David, a recent graduate, was killed in action with the Marine Corps. Another graduate, Jeanie, died of an unexplained illness. Jim, a junior, died in an automobile accident. (The police suspected suicide.) "Miss Chip," a phys. ed. teacher, died of cancer. Diana, a freshman, was found brutally murdered in a field next to the school.

Needless to say, these deaths raised many of the same questions in my mind that were expressed in my recent survey. To find the answers, I went to people who confront death on a daily basis. I talked with doctors and intensive care nurses as I tagged along during a hospital shift. I spoke with patients who had "out-of-body experiences" while just inches from death. I rode "shotgun" with a police officer who has investigated teen murders and suicides (and who let me read actual suicide notes). A funeral director allowed me to witness the embalming of a body. I interviewed a school counselor who dealt with teens following deaths of several classmates. I talked with the parents of a girl who killed herself at 15. I spoke with a mother who lost a son to AIDS and a daughter to a murderer. And I talked with ministers who attempt to provide answers—or at least hope—during the funerals of young people.

During the 10 months I spent investigating death, I discovered more questions than answers. So you won't find a lot of pat answers and canned clichés in this book. What you will find are honest people who have stared death in the face yet have lived through the emotions of grief. In the process, they've discovered God holding them up even when they don't have all the answers. I trust you will too.

Dear friend, I pray that you may enjoy good health and that all may go well with you, even as your soul is getting along well. (3 John 2)

Jim Watkins

Part ONE

What Is Death Like?

It's a miracle that I lived to write this book!

As a kid, I tried to make **rocket fuel** out of gasoline. Jumped car ramps with my bike. Tried parachuting off the garage roof with an umbrella. Spent considerable time in the emergency room for assorted stitches. And watched a tornado lift up the neighbor's garage.

1 How Many Teens Die Each Year?

In high school, I ended up on the bottom of a pile of teens when a wagon tipped over during a hayride. I tried to ride my unicycle with Kim Williams on my shoulders. (We did really well until both of us suddenly wondered, *How do we get off!?* With a lot of pain!) And I rode to school with Cal "I-bet-I-can-take-that-turn-at-60" Algier. (We didn't, but we did make a great **360** in the intersection.)

Later, I flew with an Alaskan bush pilot who commented before takeoff, "We're about 50 pounds overweight, but I *think* we can clear those pine trees at the end of the runway." I've ridden with **kamikaze** pilots turned Bombay taxi drivers and driven through downtown Chicago—at rush hour—in a motor home during a snowstorm. I've nearly drowned trying to rescue a teen swimmer. (I would have done fine if his friend hadn't panicked and grabbed me around the neck from behind.) And I've wrestled with a teen who was trying to commit suicide by jumping off a second-story balcony.

Like I said, it's a miracle I'm alive to write a book about death.

And it's a miracle that *you're* alive to read it! Nearly **one-third** of all children die before birth because of abortions.[1]

According to the latest statistics from the *Statistical Abstract of the United States,* the odds of dying at birth are 1/105 for white males and 1/52 for black males, 1/134 for white females, and 1/62 for black females. (In other words, one black female baby will die at birth for every 62 black female babies born.)[2] And the odds for dying before we reach our teen years are 1/74 for white males and 1/40 for black males, 1/96 for white females and 1/47 for black females.

So we've overcome some tough odds just to get to this chapter!

What's the main cause of teen deaths?

The following charts reveal just how young people ages 15–24 die each year.

How Many Teens Die Each Year?		
CAUSE	MALE	FEMALE
Accident	10,313	3,529
Murder	6,224	1,060
Suicide	4,132	652
AIDS	377	252
Cancer	1,009	633
Heart failure	659	380
Other diseases	607	470
Total	**25,777**	**8,467**

Source: Statistical Abstract of the United States, 1998

What Are Your Odds?

CAUSE	MALE	FEMALE
Accident	1/1,901	1/5,555
Murder	1/2,950	1/17,322
Suicide	—	—
AIDS	—	—
Cancer	1/18,182	1/28,982
Heart failure	1/27,778	1/48,173
Other diseases	1/32,000	1/55,495
Total	**1/711**	**1/2,165**

Source: Statistical Abstract of the United States, 1998

What are your chances of getting murdered?

Before getting too depressed as you look at those statistics, keep in mind that 99.86 percent of young men from 15–24 years of age **will not die** this year; 99.95 percent of young women in the same age range will not die this year. As you can see on the "odds chart," your chances of dying in an accident are pretty low, and the probability of dying of cancer or heart disease is lower yet.

If you're an African American young man between the ages of 15 and 19, your chances of being killed by gunfire are greater than any other cause of death according to the National Center for Health Statistics. In Los Angeles and Washington D.C., the odds against you are 1/444. In New York City, your odds are better: 1/1,000.

However, students are twice as likely to be struck by **lightning** than by bullets in school.[3]

In the case of suicide and AIDS, you can pretty much determine your own odds.

WHAT IS DEATH LIKE?

And as you'll discover in chapter 3, you can dramatically better your chances of living long enough to have the president send you a card on your **100th** birthday.

Despite the good odds, however, teens *do* die—more than 34,000 in the United States each year! Chances are that not only will you experience the death of an elderly relative, but you'll also be confronted with the death of a teenage friend sometime during junior high or high school.

My hope and prayer is that this book will help you in **t w o** ways:

1. It will give you information that will allow you, as much as is humanly possible, to understand God's **gift of life** and develop skills to live a long, healthy life.

2. Along with your faith in Christ, it will give you **comfort and hope** as you deal with family and friends who won't live a long, healthy life.

Bill sits beneath the blinding lights in the TV studio. The skin on his face hangs like the rippled curtains behind him, and spotlights reflect off his bald head. He pushes himself back in the chair with thin, wrinkled arms and hands, then rubs his back, which is disfigured from arthritis. As he begins to talk, his

2 What's the Cause of Death?

voice is weak and sometimes hard to understand because of several missing teeth. Bill is 12 years old!

Yes, 12. He's a guest on a talk show featuring a little-known disease called Werner's Syndrome—premature aging. Bill's body will race through childhood, adolescence, and old age within a few decades. He'll probably die of "old age" before he's 40.

Doctors and researchers are particularly anxious to know what causes this rare form of aging. And if they do discover its causes, they may discover the answer to an **age-old** question:

Why do people die?

Theories of why we fall apart fall into two categories: wear and tear and planned obsolescence.[4]

Our cells busily reproduce themselves throughout our lifetime. During all this multiplying and dividing of protein, our **DNA** (our genetic blueprint) occasionally makes a mistake. Scientists speculate that exposure to toxins (poisons in our environment), chemicals, and ultraviolet light breaks, twists, or scrambles these genetic codes. Thus, occasional "factory defects" roll off our cell assembly lines.

When enough bad products accumulate, cells begin to break down and our bodies begin to show signs of aging. The chart below shows how our bodies lose efficiency over the years. At 100 percent efficiency, our bodies would work perfectly at maximum power; at 0 percent efficiency—well, you wouldn't be reading this book.

Age	25	45	65	86
Muscles	100%	90%	75%	55%
Heart	100%	94%	87%	81%
Lungs	100%	82%	62%	50%
Kidneys	100%	88%	78%	69%
Cholesterol	198	221	224	206

Now you know why there are so few professional athletes older than 40! With age, athletes—and everyone else—lose muscle strength and lung capacity and experience a decrease in heart and kidney effectiveness as well.

One cause of wear and tear may be blood sugar, called *glucose*. High levels of glucose can cause protein cells to stick together in a **gooey mess.** These globs of protein and glucose can cloud over your eyes, clog arteries, gum up kidney function, and make breathing difficult.

Scientists discovered this aging suspect while studying diabetics. People with diabetes have higher than normal blood sugar levels and one-third lower life expectancy than nondiabetics. (Incidentally, switching to NutraSweet or giving up sugar altogether has no observable effect.)

Mice and rats that were fed 40 percent fewer calories than the rodents in neighboring cages at the National Toxology Laboratory lived twice as long. Physiologist Edward Masoro believes the slimmer diet produced less glucose, thus less goo, and, finally, less chance of premature death.

Our bodies' immunity systems produce cells called *macrophages,* which are sent out on "seek and destroy" missions against these sticky glucose bonds. The dieting rats also had more of these macrophage **goo chewers.** But for some yet unknown reason, these goo gobblers become less efficient as we age.

Not only do we get sticky and gooey, we also RUST with age! Oxygen and "free radicals" allegedly cause protein to rust much the same way rain and snow cause a car to fall apart. Free radicals were first introduced by Denham Harman of the University of Nebraska. The burning of oxygen in cells produces these mutant molecules that stalk our bodies, destroying fats and proteins. Exposure to sunlight, X-rays, ozone, tobacco smoke, and air pollution are also suspects in the creation of those molecular muggers.

Harman's fellow researchers blame free radicals for destructive diseases such as arthritis, diabetes, hardening of the arteries, heart and kidney failure, lung disease, and cancer.

Don't we start dying as soon as we're born?

Planned obsolescence means that a product is designed to self-destruct in a certain number of years. (Have you noticed that as soon as your CD player's warranty expires so does your CD player?) Some researchers believe that our bodies are made the same way—we are programmed to **self-destruct** after about 70 years.

But this wasn't God's plan when He created the first people. God created Adam and Eve to live, and the presence of the tree of life in the Garden of Eden suggests that if they ate its fruit, they would have **lived forever.** No obsolescence. Then Adam and Eve sinned by eating the fruit of the tree of the knowledge of good and evil. The result of that sin is death—not just for them, but for all human beings. God didn't plan it—Adam, Eve, and each of us bring it on ourselves. But who would want to live eternally in a sinful world anyway? However, God, in His grace, has turned death into a gateway to a perfect life with Christ in heaven—forever.

Despite the advances of modern science, people are not living any longer than the proposed 70-year genetic "guarantee" allowed people to live centuries ago. Today, more people are simply living. For instance, if two people die at childbirth and two people live to be 70, then the average life span is 35. If only one person dies in infancy and three reach 70, the life expectancy jumps to 52. And if all four make it to retirement, then the average life span springboards to 70! But not one person has lived any longer—**m o r e** have simply lived to reach 70.

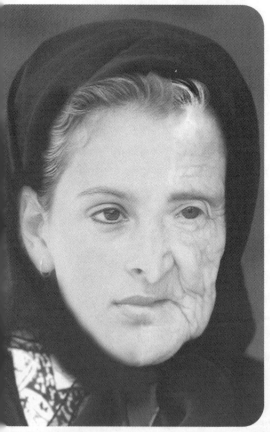

What is the longest you can live?

Scientists claim that the longest possible lifetime is between 115 and 120 years. But that's nothing new. The book of Genesis states the limit is "a hundred and twenty years" (Genesis 6:3). (We'll talk about 969-year-old Methuselah later.) The ancient Roman, Pliny the Elder, wrote about 100-year-old people. Shigechiyo Izumi of Japan, the oldest person in recent history, lived to the ripe old age of—you guessed it—**120!**

According to statistics, guys born in 1990 can expect to live to 76.1 years and girls to 83.4, with many living long enough to light 100 candles on their birthday cake. But why can't we break the 120-year barrier? Scientists claim the answer is "genetics." And since identical twins, who have identical genes, have very similar natural life expectancies, scientists claim that we are programmed by our DNA to self-destruct at a certain age.

In the same way that our bodies change during adolescence, some researchers believe we begin to fall apart on some genetic cue. For instance, between the ages of 14 and 70, our immune system—which fights off disease—decreases by 90 percent. Microbiologist Leonard Hayflick is even more fatalistic. In 1964, he discovered that human cells seem to divide only 50 times, then die. Fifty times and no more!

Other researchers, like the University of Colorado's Thomas Johnson, believe that the exact gene for long life can be isolated. Right now his research is with WORMS, but he believes he's located the gene that makes the difference between long- and short-lived fishing bait. And UCLA researcher Roy Walford may be the first genetic engineer to lengthen life. He's attempting to transfer genes from 8-year-old mice into shorter-living rodents.

How come people lived longer during Bible times?

If 120 years seems to be the maximum life span for humans, how do we justify biblical accounts of people living nearly 1,000 years? The fifth chapter of Genesis claims Adam lived to celebrate 930 birthdays. Methuselah, however, had 969 candles on this cake!

Some biblical scholars offer an interesting theory: In the creation account, it appears that the earth was covered with a **greenhouse** covering of water: "And God said, 'Let there be an expanse between the waters to separate water from water.' So God made the expanse and separated the water under the expanse from the water above it. And it was so. God called the expanse 'sky'" (Genesis 1:6–8a). It appears that high above the sky, a shield of water protected the earth from the sun's radiation.

Later, in the account of the flood, Moses reports, "All the springs of the great deep burst forth, and the floodgates of the heavens were opened" (Genesis 7:11). The first rains fell, and the greenhouse canopy was destroyed. As we noted earlier, the sun's ultraviolet rays are thought to be a factor in the aging process. Is it possible that this "RADIA-TION SHIELD" came crashing down from the heavens? Without the protection, we could expect much shorter life spans. And sure enough, the life spans begin to shorten in future chapters of Genesis: Noah's son Shem lived to be "only" 500; Abraham lived to be 170; Joseph lived to be 110.

Whether the aging process is "wear and tear" or "planned obsolescence" (Romans 6:23), we don't need to be fatalistic—"When my number's up, my number's up!" Diet, exercise, and other factors (which we'll discuss in the next chapter) can delay the aging process. God wants us to use these tools to take good care of our bodies so we can serve Him in full health.

In an underground storage site near Los Angeles, human beings are being **frozen solid** in giant thermos bottles! The reason: hope for eternal life.

At the instant of death, these terminally ill patients are wrapped in aluminum foil, then stored in liquid

3 What Are Some Ways to Avoid Death?

nitrogen in giant containers. They hope that when a treatment is found for their fatal disease, they'll be defrosted and cured.

The idea of *cryogenic suspension* isn't new. In 1626 the English philosopher Francis Bacon first attempted the process by stuffing a chicken with snow. The experiment with eternal life was deadly. Bacon caught cold and died soon afterward! However, more recently, scientists began storing fresh blood in liquid nitrogen. The blood cells, if first soaked in an antifreeze agent, can be stored indefinitely at **-320°F.**

With this success as inspiration, the first human was put into cold storage at a Los Angeles company in

1967. The cost of dying to live again is a bit frosty: starting at $15,000 in cold cash. Plus there's a $1,000-per-year charge for "locker rental."

Scientists are skeptical about the success of putting people on ice. Cryogenic research has not found a way to freeze the entire brain quickly enough to save vital cells. So much for living forever as an **ice cube.**

Are there any secrets to living longer?

There are some proven ways, however, to extend your life. Former Secretary of Health, Education, and Welfare, Joseph Califano Jr., claims "67 percent of all disease and premature death is preventable."[5] Dr. Peter Greenwald of the National Cancer Institute says that "80 percent of cancer cases are linked to how we live our lives," so we can avoid the deadly disease eight out of 10 times.[6]

Here's how to live longer:

- Eat your Cheerios.
- Keep off extra pounds.
- Walk, don't drive, to school/work.
- Kick butts.
- Get married; remain faithful.
- Move to Hawaii.

Maybe I'd better explain those suggestions!

Are you really what you eat?!

Okay, if you eat your body weight at Pizza Hut's lunch buffet, you're not going to look like a Meat Lovers pizza. And if you simply nibble at the salad bar, you're not going to look like SWAMP THING. But your body does need healthy food to remain healthy.

Six major nutrients act as building blocks for a healthy body:

1. **Carbohydrates**—These nutrients come in the form of sugar and starch, which breaks down into sugar. These sugars provide fuel for our bodies. Bread, cereal, spaghetti, noodles, popcorn, and rice make up this category. Whole-grain breads and cereals contain fiber that keeps us regular and acts to prevent colorectal cancer. Fiber also may help reduce the "bad" cholesterol that clogs up our arteries.

2. **Protein**—Muscles, skin, hair, blood cells, and bones are mostly protein, which we get from milk, meat, eggs, cheese, nuts, beans, peas, and other protein-rich foods.

   Many researchers believe to live healthier, we must reduce the amount of red meat (which is thought to increase the bad cholesterol) and increase our intake of fish, chicken, and turkey. Instead of fried meat, eat boiled, broiled, or baked foods.

   The popular "Protein Power" diet, developed by Drs. Michael and Mary Eades, suggests that we need more protein in our diets and less carbohydrates to lower weight and cholesterol.[7] (Carbohydrates turn to sugars, which increase insulin production, which slows down metabolism and adds extra insulation.)

3. **Vitamins**—Vitamin A contributes to good vision. Vitamin B keeps our nerves, muscles, and skin in good shape. Vitamin C, along with vitamin E and beta carotene (the vegetable parent of vitamin A), is thought to protect us from those nasty "free radicals" from chapter 2 that cause us to "rust." Vitamin D helps heal wounds and broken bones. Vitamin E keeps our skin smooth and may even boost our immune system. Vegetables, fruit, and milk are good sources of many vitamins.

4. **Minerals**—Calcium and iron are two important nutrients. Calcium, found in milk, builds strong bones and teeth. Iron builds up our blood

and reduces feelings of fatigue. Sources of iron include fish, chicken, turkey, lean red meat, and leafy green vegetables.

5. **Water**—Our bodies are made up of about 80 percent water, so it's a very important part of our diet. Doctors suggest you drink eight eight-ounce glasses of H_2O per day.

6. **Fat**—Despite the bad rap it's gotten recently, fat is an essential nutrient. It provides energy, transports vitamins throughout the body, keeps us warm in cold weather, and acts as a shock absorber for the internal organs. However, we don't need as much fat in our diet as most of us take in. (Sorry, Oreos are *not* considered a basic food group!) Most of us can get by on less fat than we pack away into storage. By maintaining our ideal weight, we lower our chances of high blood pressure and heart disease.

Here's what the American Medical Association recommends as ideal weight based on height. (Height is without shoes; weight is without clothes.)

Height	Men	Women
4'10"	—	92–119
4'11"	—	94–122
5'	—	96–125
5'1"	—	99–128
5'2"	112–141	102–131
5'3"	115–144	105–134
5'4"	118–148	108–138
5'5"	121–152	111–142
5'6"	124–156	114–146
5'7"	128–161	118–150
5'8"	132–166	122–154
5'9"	136–170	126–158
5'10"	140–174	130–163
5'11"	144–179	134–168
6'	148–184	138–173
6'1"	152–189	—
6'2"	156–194	—
6'3"	160–199	—
6'4"	164–204	—

Most researchers claim we get most of our nutrients by eating the following each day:

- Two servings of meat, fish, or poultry
- Three to four servings of dairy products
  ## (Sorry, Dairy Queen Blizzards don't count!)
- One serving each of vegetable and fruit (The National Institute of Nutrition suggests five servings of each.)
- Four servings of bread or cereal

Eating right and getting plenty of exercise usually will keep our bodies in good shape. If you still feel weak or are having a hard time with your weight, check with your school nurse or family doctor. They should be able to give you some helpful suggestions.

How can you keep looking young?

As I was slouched in front of the TV with my bag of Oreos, this ad caught my attention:

Europe's Miracle Body Shaper

"FIGURE-TRON II"

For Those Vital Figure-toning Wonders of

3,000 Sit-ups without Moving an Inch

10 Miles of Jogging Lying Flat on Your Back

For just $19.95 (plus $3.00 postage and handling), the announcer promised that I could wire myself up to "Unitronic" electrodes as "tiny micro-electronic impulses tone your muscles *500 times a minute!* Automatically works on slack, flabby muscles in just *15 minutes a day!* All you do is lie there—amazing Figure-Tron II tones your body's sag spots. *It's like hours of exercise in just a few minutes' time!* Literally dial in a more youthful-looking, more beautiful, body."

And, of course, there was the model with the *youthful-looking, more beautiful, body!*

The Federal Food and Drug Administration claims the Body Shaper is a fraud and that regular exercise will keep us younger longer than wasting $19.95 on a 9-volt battery and some electrodes. As the old **Nike commercials** told us,

"Just Do It." (I did buy a NordicTrack, which simulates cross-country skiing. It has helped me shed some weight and build up my heart and lungs. Not all "exercise equipment" ads are scams, but if it looks too good to be true, it probably is.)

The American Medical Association makes the following three recommendations:

1. At least three times a week, have an **exercise period** that lasts 20 minutes or more with little or no pause for rest. Doctors recommend that we choose activities that make us feel "breathless, sweaty, and aware of our heart beating." They warn, however, not to do anything so stressful that it makes us "dizzy or nauseated, or risk straining muscles or joints." Always do warm-ups before

and a cool-down after any exercise. (And my lawyer wants me to tell you, consult your family physician before starting any exercise program!)

2. Choose **enjoyable exercises** that fit into your schedule. The goal is to develop a lifelong habit of physical fitness—not just strenuous spring training to try to squeeze into last year's swimsuit.

3. Take your **t i m e .** Our bodies don't get out of shape overnight and, unfortunately, they don't get back into shape any sooner.

The following is the AMA's analysis of various exercises. The "Calories" column shows how many units are burned in 20 minutes of that activity. The "Heart/Lungs," "Flexibility," and "Strength" columns note benefits in these areas. Like movie reviews, a rating of four stars is excellent; one star means the exercise is of minimal benefit.[8]

Activity	Calories	Heart/Lungs	Flexibility	Strength
Easy Walking	60	*	*	*
Golf	90	*	*	*
Brisk Walking	100	**	*	**
Gymnastics	140	**	***	**
Dancing	160	**	***	*
Easy Jogging	160	**	*	**
Tennis	160	***	***	**
Downhill Skiing	160	****	***	***
Cross-Country Skiing	180	****	***	***
Soccer	180	***	***	***
Football	180	***	**	***
Racquetball	200	***	***	**
Brisk Jogging	210	****	**	***
Bicycling	220	****	**	***
Swimming	240	****	****	****

It's absolutely essential to check with your doctor before beginning an exercise plan **if** you are overweight, a smoker, or under treatment for high blood pressure; heart, lung, or kidney disease; or diabetes.

The rest of you, "Drop and give me 10 push-ups!" (It sure beats pushing up daisies.)

Will smoking really kill you?

According to a 1998 study by the Centers for Disease Control and Prevention, smoking rates among students are on the rise—increasing by nearly a third from 27.5 percent in 1991 to 36.4 percent in 1997. Nearly half (48.2 percent) of male students and more than a third (36 percent) of female students reported using some form of tobacco—cigarette, cigar, or smokeless tobacco—in the past month. Among African American students, whose low smoking rates over the past decade have been a public health success story, past-month cigarette smoking rates increased by an estimated 80 percent from 1991 to 1997.

Many teens think smoking will make them look more mature. That's right, and that's the problem. Smoking ages a person physically! One study reveals that the CARBON MONOXIDE in smoke deprives your face of oxygen, increasing wrinkles and complexion problems.

But that's nothing compared with what smoking does to your life expectancy! Smoking killed 434,000 people in the United States last year. That's more than the entire population of Chattanooga, Tennessee, or nearly the entire population of Wyoming! It's the single most preventable cause of death in the United States.

What makes smoking so dangerous? There are enough chemicals in burning tobacco to start your own hazardous landfill—4,027 in all. More than 200 of them are known poisons and 16 are known to cause cancer.

- **Carbon monoxide,** found in cigarette smoke, is identical to automotive exhaust! (Your bloodstream carries CO better than O_2, so it can be deadly to put CO into your system.)

- **Hydrogen cyanide,** used to execute criminals in gas chambers, is found in cigarette smoke.

- Recent studies have shown that cigarette smoke is radioactive and actually can create "hot spots" in lungs. (The people smoking up the school bathrooms may be more hazardous to your health than living next door to a nuclear power plant.)

- **Tar** in cigarettes is virtually identical to the black coating on the mall parking lot. (One year of smoking can produce a quart of blacktop sealant in a smoker's lungs.)

- Perhaps the most dangerous chemical is nicotine. This extremely addictive drug is both a stimulant and a depressant. In fact, it's one of the few drugs that has absolutely no medical benefit because it acts so unpredictably. Some researchers even claim that nicotine is more addictive than heroin or cocaine because only one out of three who seriously try to kick the smoking habit are able to do so.

If you smoke, here are some suggestions that may work for you as you try to **quit.**

1. "Get with the program." There are many free stop-smoking programs available including:

"The Seven-Day Quitter's Guide" The American Cancer Society 3340 Peachtree NE Atlanta, GA 30326	The American Lung Association P.O. Box 596DN New York, NY 10001	The National Cancer Institute 1-800-4-CANCER

If self-help programs don't work, see your doctor. He or she can offer many new medical treatments and drugs (nicotine gum, nicotine patches, etc.) that can help reduce the **craving** for a smoke.

2. Don't buy cigarettes. Don't carry a lighter or matches. If you have to constantly bum cigarettes and lights, it may be more difficult to smoke.

3. Tell your friends you're quitting and ask for their help to keep you accountable. Spend time with friends who **don't smoke.**

4. When the urge to smoke hits, take a deep breath. Hold it for 10 seconds, then release it slowly. Taking deep, rhythmic breaths is similar to smoking, only you'll inhale clean air—not poisonous gases.

5. Get rid of smoker's breath by brushing your teeth several times. Notice how much better your mouth tastes and your breath smells!

6. Cleanse your body of nicotine. Drink lots of **water,** fruit juices, or caffeine-free soft drinks. Coffee and caffeinated soft drinks can increase your urge to smoke.

7. Exercise to help relieve tension. (If you skipped the last chapter, check it out. Hey, I know exercise is no fun, but neither is dying before 40!)

8. Eat rather than smoke—but stick to low-calorie, high-nutrition foods. Avoid spicy foods that can trigger a desire for a smoke.

9. Change habits associated with smoking. Try to **avoid** the spots where you used to smoke. (Use the school rest room only when absolutely necessary!)

10. Use the money you save by not buying cigarettes to reward yourself with something fun: a new CD, new clothes, or the first book in this series, *When Can I Start Dating?*

You'll also be rewarding yourself with better-looking skin and fewer wrinkles, increased energy and endurance, better and more restful sleep, fewer colds and infections, lower risk of lung cancer and heart disease, and a longer life.

I keep hearing about all these people killed by just drinking. That's not true, is it?

Tobacco and alcohol are the two most abused drugs in the United States—and the most deadly. **Alcohol** is the number one cause of **automobile deaths,** and half of all those killed are teens.

In addition, heavy drinking over a number of years can cause damage to the liver and pancreas; increase the risk of cancer of the mouth, larynx, esophagus, and liver; and lead to malnutrition, stomach irritation, less resistance to diseases, and irreversible damage to the brain and nervous system. On the average, a heavy drinker's life is **cut short** by 10 to 12 years!

Some people believe they can avoid these problems because they believe the following myths.

Myth #1: "Beer drinkers consume less alcohol."

While beer does have less alcohol than wine or liquor, beer drinkers don't drink any less alcohol. Beer (at 4 percent alcohol) is usually drunk in 12-ounce servings, which equal ½ ounce of alcohol. Wine (at 12 percent alcohol) is usually drunk in four-ounce servings, which equal ½ ounce of alcohol. Liquor (at "86 proof" it has 43 percent alcohol) is usually drunk in one-ounce servings, which equal—you guessed it—½ ounce of alcohol.

Myth #2: " 'Lite' beers have less alcohol."

They have fewer *calories* but not less alcohol. Unfortunately, because they're "less filling," users may end up drinking **more** than they would if drinking regular beer.

Myth #3: "Eating while drinking will keep a person from getting drunk."

Eating does slow down the rate at which alcohol is absorbed into the bloodstream, but it doesn't *prevent* alcohol's effects. As a result, a person may end up drinking too much because of the delayed reaction. This is especially dangerous because someone may feel completely sober when he leaves a party or restaurant, but the alcohol's effects can kick in with full force while he is driving home.

Myth #4: "When someone gets down to serious drinking and begins to urinate at roughly the same rate as beer is being chugged, the alcohol passes right through and has little effect on the body."

What is passing through the body is the excess water, not the alcohol. The alcohol is oxidized—or burned up—by the body at a steady rate of ⅜ of an ounce per hour. Scientists also have discovered that women's stomachs absorb more alcohol, so more alcohol gets into the bloodstream.

Myth #5: "Black coffee is the best way to sober up."

Wrong again. And forget about cold showers, fresh air, serious talk, food, exercise, or deep breathing. Once the alcohol is in the stomach, it goes straight to the bloodstream. There is nothing that will speed up the oxidation described earlier. Black coffee—because it's a stimulant—will help a drunk person wake up, but the result is not "sobering up." She is now simply a wide-awake drunk. The real danger in these "remedies" is that the drinker may be convinced she is sober while her body's alcohol content has not been remedied.

If you—or a friend—are having **problems** with alcohol (signs include missing school, getting drunk, becoming aggressive, etc.), here are some ways you can get help for yourself or your friend.

1. Learn all you can about alcoholism. The more you know, the more you can help—and the less frustrated you'll become.

2. Don't "preach," threaten, or insult the alcoholic in an effort to get him to quit drinking. He will be better motivated by **love and support** than by humiliation.

3. Don't "cover" for the alcoholic's behavior. As long as drinkers don't have to face up to the consequences of their actions when drunk, there's no motivation to quit. While it may seem cruel to let a friend spend the night passed out in her own vomit on the bathroom floor, alcoholics often must suffer some pain before there's any desire to get help. (Obviously, don't allow a friend to stay in a situation that is life-threatening, such as passed out on the sidewalk during the coldest night of winter. But if it's warm weather in a safe neighborhood, let

your friend wake up to the fact that her drinking is **out of control**.)

4. When he's ready to admit his need for help, suggest a support group such as AA (Alcoholics Anonymous). There are also groups for family members—ALATEEN for children of alcoholic parents and ALANON for husbands, wives, and relatives of alcoholics. All three programs are free and available in most cities. Or write for free information to:

National Council on Alcoholism
2875 Northwind Drive, Suite 225
East Lansing, MI 48823

Is caffeine a killer? I heard that on some talk show.

The late Dr. Patricia Mutch, former director of the Institute for Alcoholism and Drug Dependency, made headlines when she claimed caffeine was a deadly drug that caused everything from irregular heartbeats to "genetic mutations." Yikes! Too many Diet Pepsis and your kids will have fizz for brains?!

First, the bad news. Excessive caffeine intake from coffee, tea, soft drinks, and chocolate can lead to an irregular heart rate, diuresis (excessive urination), nausea and vomiting, restlessness, depression, tremors, and difficulty sleeping.

Now, the good news. A 1984 statement from the American Medical Association Council on Scientific Affairs concluded: "Moderate tea or coffee drinkers probably have no concern for their health relative to their caffeine consumption provided other lifestyle habits are moderate as well."[9]

So enjoy the Diet Pepsi, but keep moderation in mind. Caffeine can make you more alert, but it doesn't improve your memory, comprehension, or other abilities.

Obviously, caffeine and coffins don't have a direct connection, but everything you can do to avoid unnecessary risks increases your chances of living longer. **Drugs,** on the other hand, have been proven D(ADLY.

- "Coke" is one of the most widely used illegal drugs and one of the most addictive. Heavy users must increase dosages to get the same effect and those effects include death. Cocaine can cause cold sweats, dizziness, chest pain, heart problems, vomiting, uncontrollable shaking, loss of sleep, and weight loss. The number of reported deaths, which result from multiple seizures followed by heart and lung failure, is steadily increasing.

- **Inhalants** are a growing problem as well. I got my first lecture on huffing in second grade when I was building a model of a Tom Cat fighter plane. "James Norman Watkins, that airplane glue will rot your brains out if you don't open a window." It turned out that Mom and Dad were

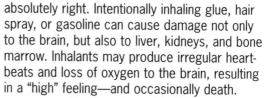

absolutely right. Intentionally inhaling glue, hair spray, or gasoline can cause damage not only to the brain, but also to liver, kidneys, and bone marrow. Inhalants may produce irregular heartbeats and loss of oxygen to the brain, resulting in a "high" feeling—and occasionally death.

- Marijuana users claim "POT" is a "safe" drug, but research has shown opposite results. Because marijuana smokers inhale more deeply and hold the smoke in longer, its use is much more dangerous to lungs than regular cigarettes. And pot smoke contains even more cancer-causing ingredients than tobacco.

- Methamphetamine is commonly known as "speed," "meth," and "chalk." In its smoked form, it is often referred to as "ice," "crystal," "crank," and "glass." It is a white, odorless, bitter-tasting crystalline powder that easily dissolves in water or alcohol. Like its weaker brother, amphetamine, it causes increased activity, decreased appetite, and a general sense of well being. After the initial "rush," there is typically a state of high agitation that in some individuals can lead to violent behavior.

According to the National Institute on Drug Abuse, heavy speed users exhibit violent behavior, anxiety, confusion, and insomnia. They also can experience paranoia ("People are trying to harm me!"), hearing voices, mood disturbances, and delusions (for example, the sensation of insects creeping on the skin). Severe paranoia can result in homicidal as well as suicidal thoughts.

This stimulant is easily made in a homemade lab, but the production process creates a strong odor. For this reason, the "meth labs" have moved from coastal urban centers to the rural Midwest.

- PCP, called "**angel dust**" or "super pot," is potentially deadly because it gives users the feeling that they are all-powerful and that nothing can hurt them. PCP users have jumped from tall buildings, believing they could fly; they have burned to death because they could feel no pain; and they often have become violent and destructive to others and themselves.

- Anabolic s t e r o i d s—the synthetic version of the male hormone testosterone—have been used illegally to build muscle and strength in both male and female athletes and bodybuilders. Although steroids are effective, especially for female athletes, they have some deadly side effects. They build not only muscles but tumors. They can cause heart disease, liver damage, and hormonal imbalance.

Side effects of anabolic steroids in men include prostate cancer, shrinking testicles, and enlarged breasts; in women, the side effects include a lower voice, more facial hair, shrinking breasts, and even baldness. Steroid use can lead to aggressiveness (called "roid rage"), depression, and mental illness, including hallucinations and "hearing voices."

East German athlete Birgit Dressel (26 years old), New Zealand discus thrower Robin Tait (40), and NFL football player Lyle Alzado (43) all reportedly have died as a direct result of steroid abuse. Because steroids are illegal, many other professional and amateur athletes are suspected to have died of steroid use, but doctors and family members have kept the cause of death secret.

- Other potentially deadly drugs include amphetamines ("uppers"), barbiturates ("downers"), heroin, and LSD ("acid").

Sorry for the temperance lecture, but several of you wanted to know how to live longer. And drug abuse is a proven way to schedule an early funeral. Okay, let's get to the good stuff …

Is there any way to live longer?

If you want to double your chances of a long life, **get married.** That's the conclusion of several university studies.[10] Researchers tracked 8,000 middle-aged men in Sweden. At the end of 10 years, 9 percent of the married men had died, but 20 percent of the single men had died. A similar study in Finland adjusted its results to account for tobacco use, cholesterol levels, and blood pressure. Even taking these factors into consideration, the married men still outlived single men two to one.

These findings also have been verified in the United States. Robert H. Coombs of the UCLA School of Medicine has confirmed that "married people live longer and generally are more emotionally and physically healthy than the unmarried. The

therapeutic **benefit** of marriage remains relatively unrecognized."[11]

In 1987, Debra Umberson found that both men and women live longer if married than single and that those men and women who are married with children had the best survival rates. She concludes that those with the responsibility of a spouse and children tend to avoid destructive behaviors such as "excessive drinking, drug use, risk-taking, and disorderly living."[12]

Even when they do face life-threatening illness, married people have better rates of survival. A Michigan Cancer Foundation study concluded "marriage influences survivorship among cancer patients."[13] Perhaps the support of a spouse—and a desire to **survive** for his or her sake—contributes to survival rates.

Of course, merely saying "I do" will not add years to your life. But those who are willing to make a lifelong commitment tend to live longer by avoiding destructive behaviors. There's also some real health "assurance" in remaining sexually pure before marriage and sexually faithful to your spouse after the honeymoon. I've written about the potentially deadly aspects of promiscuity in the first book in this series, *When Can I Start Dating?*, so I'll just mention that at least two of the 40 STDs (sexually transmitted diseases) can mean RIP (Rest in Peace).

Where you live also can increase or decrease your life expectancy. According to the National Center for Health Statistics, Hawaiians have the longest life expectancy at 77.02 years. In addition to Hawaii, the **Top Ten** list includes Minnesota (76.15), Iowa (75.81), Utah (75.81), North Dakota (75.71), Nebraska (75.49), Wisconsin (75.35), Kansas (75.31), Colorado (75.3), and Idaho (75.19).

The **10 worst** places to live—if you want to live long—are the District of

Columbia (69.2), Louisiana (71.74), South Carolina (71.85), Mississippi (71.98), Georgia (72.22), Alaska (72.24), Alabama (72.53), Nevada (72.64), West Virginia (72.84), and North Carolina (72.96).

Many factors contribute to the life expectancy of a particular location (crime rates, public health care, poverty level, etc.), so simply moving to **Hawaii** is no guarantee—but it sure couldn't hurt!

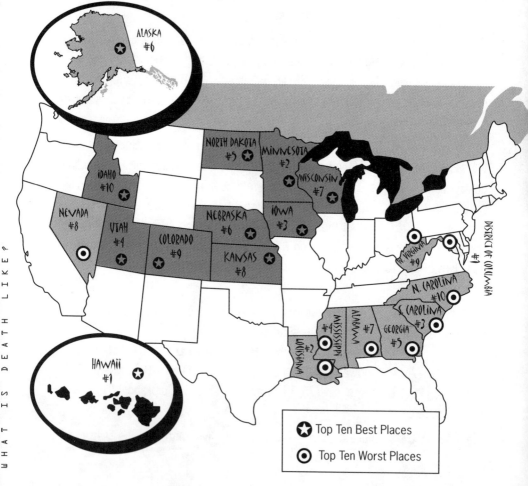

Part TWO

How Can a Person Deal with Death?

How can a person deal with death? I'd like to introduce you to six friends who stare into the chalky face of death on a daily basis.

Ron Sloan is a medical doctor who specializes in family practice. During his career, he's held dead babies in his hands, told teens they have leukemia,

How Can You Deal with Accidents and Terminal Illnesses?

and performed CPR on patients who never revived. Tina Bowen and Charlene Baungartner are registered nurses who specialize in **intensive care** and emergency room nursing. We'll meet these three people in just a few moments.

In the next chapter, I'll introduce you to Jerry Custer, captain of a small town **police** department. He's personally dealt with three murders, four attempted murders, and 17 suicides. He says he's lost count of the fatal auto accidents he's witnessed or investigated.

In chapter 6, we'll meet young people who have seen their friends and classmates gunned down in their school. Some carry the physical (bullet) as well as emotional wounds of the tragedy.

And in chapter 8, we'll meet Jim and Mike Stone, who are funeral directors. They allowed me to observe the embalming of an elderly woman's body, and we also talked about **funerals** of young people.

First, though, here's how the medical community deals with death.

Do doctors and nurses get used to death?

Tina and Charlene spend most of their eight-hour shift watching oscilloscope screens that monitor the heart rates of six patients who are, more or less, close to death. Electrical sensors are glued to each patient's chest and sides and pick up the contractions and relaxations of the heart muscle. The RHYTHM of this muscle activity is depicted graphically on a TV monitor.

Suddenly the yellow alarm light flashes and an alarm sounds on monitor four as a printer wildly pens closely spaced peaks and valleys. Tina calmly picks up the phone and calls the nurses' station. "Hi, this is Tina. What is Mr. Trombley doing? We've got a strange pattern."

As Tina waits while a nurse checks on the patient, Charlene explains the pattern. "It's not a heart pattern. It could be a SEIZURE, but it's more likely not. But something's going on with a lot of muscle action."

Charlene pulls off the narrow strip of paper and studies it. "I'm guessing he's brushing his teeth. See, you can see the consistent up and down motion that the heart monitor is picking up."

Tina continues to wait patiently for an answer. "Okay, that was one of our choices—that or a seizure," she says, laughing as she hangs up the phone. "Yep, he was brushing his **teeth**. This happens every mealtime—all the alarms go off, and it's everybody brushing their teeth."

I'm amazed at how casually Tina and Charlene react to abnormal rhythms on the monitors.

"You learn not to make assumptions," Tina explains. "And you learn that most of the time the alarms are for harmless body movement or perhaps a wire to the sensors has come loose. For instance, a 'flat line' that shows no **rhythm**—like you see on TV—rarely means a patient is dying. It usually means that there's an electrical problem with the machine; an electrode has come loose; the conducting gel that holds the sensors on the patient has dried out; or, if the patient is obese, that we're not getting a good reading.

"That's why we keep the in-room monitors turned away from the patient and family. Watching it just makes them nervous, and they start misinterpreting bodily movements for heart rhythms. They think, 'Oh my God, I'm dying!' when an electrode comes loose."

But Tina and Charlene are ready for any real **emergency**. Each room in the intensive care unit is filled with high-tech equipment: automatic blood pressure monitors; electrocardiogram (EKG) and respiration (breathing) monitors; oxygen tubing; suction pumps for lungs, stomachs, and body cavities to keep fluids from building up; intravenous (IV) pumps that can give continuous low doses of medications directly into a vein; a call button to summon a nurse; a code blue (emergency) button; and, of course, a cable TV remote.

Taped to the wall are variously sized airways (tubes that are inserted into the throat to deliver oxygen) and bite sticks that are put in a patient's mouth during a seizure to keep him from biting his tongue.

Each room's supply cupboard contains disposable gloves, goggles, masks, gowns, and aprons. "We're really cautious about body fluids," Tina explains, "and especially now with the 𝐝𝐚𝐧𝐠𝐞𝐫 of AIDS and hepatitis B."

In the nurses' station, a crash cart sits poised for a code blue—a stoppage of breathing and heartbeat. On top of the bright red tool chest on wheels sit the

defibrillators. "When patients go into 'V-fib,' the heart just 'fibrillates,' or quivers, rather than beating. These paddles send an electrical SHOCK through the heart and hopefully restore the heartbeat. We have to test it each shift to make sure it's working right." Tina explains.

The crash cart drawers contain medications, IV tubes in all sizes from infant to adult, and a manual suction pump. "The pump is pretty neat, but I've never had to use it, thank God," Tina comments. Both nurses say a prayer of thanks at the end of their eight-hour shift that they never had to use any of the equipment.

While Tina claims that "death is a natural part of life," medical staff—like the rest of us—want to avoid it. Charlene comments, "There used to be an old superstition in nursing that if you tied a knot in the patient's sheet, they wouldn't die on your shift. So if you see a nurse **tie a knot in your sheet**—it's not good!" They both laugh.

What goes through a person's mind who is dying?

Elisabeth Kübler-Ross, author of *On Death and Dying*, believes that the terminally ill—and their families and friends—pass through **five stages** when dealing with death: denial, anger, bargaining, depression, and acceptance.[14] Not everyone agrees with the order of these stages, and some believe people may repeat stages, but most agree these five feelings are experienced by the patient, family and friends, and medical staff. Even Christians go through these stages. Therefore, it is important that we don't assume a person's anger—even with God—means a lack of faith.

Denial

"Denial is something we physicians have to guard against," Ron Sloan, a family physician, notes over breakfast in the hospital cafeteria. "For instance, when I'm examining a pre-born's size or heart tones, I may discover something that's not quite right. There's a tendency to say to myself, 'Everything is going to be okay.' And denial isn't bad. It keeps me going through the day as I have 20 more patients to see. I don't have the emotional energy to worry about the death of a pre-born. I put it out of my mind while I'm waiting for further test results. If I started the grieving process every time I was highly suspicious, I'd do a lot of **unnecessary** grieving."

Tina agrees. "Professionally, you almost cut yourself off. That sounds really callous, but you do care. You're concerned, but then again, you can't allow yourself to feel the pain. If you get into the grieving mode, you lose your professional effectiveness. Working in the **ER** [emergency room] in suburban Chicago was really difficult. There was no chaplain, so if a multiple-injury accident came in and the doctors were busy, I was the one who had to tell the family."

Ron adds, "You have to tell people gradually to help them through the denial stage. I might say, 'You have a mass in your lung that I'm concerned about. It may be nothing, but it could be something serious.' I plant the idea that this could be a major problem, but I always give **hope**.

"Then a short time later with results, I'll say, 'This looks like it could be cancer,' but I don't say, 'You're dying.' Maybe after four meetings and additional testing I gradually give them more information—'This could be a terminal problem.' By then—many, many times—they already know it. They'll say, 'I was afraid it would be' or 'I kinda expected it.'"

In the case of a **sudden death,** Ron, like most doctors, slowly reveals the facts, rather than hitting surviving family members with all the information all at once. "Often I'm in the process of trying to revive the patient with CPR," Ron continues. "I go out to the family as soon as I can and let them know the status because they're going crazy wondering what's going on. I say something like, 'We're doing everything we can, but it doesn't look good.'

"I may continue CPR for four or five minutes—even though I know there's no chance for survival—to give the family that time for the possibility of death to sink in. I try to give the family at least some warning before I have to tell them their loved one has died."

In the case of terminal illness, the denial process can be lengthy.

Why don't people want to talk about death?

"The dying patient doesn't talk about his death because he doesn't want to put stress on the family. And his family doesn't talk about it because they don't want to create trauma for the patient," Ron explains.

"So my job is to try to break that major communication barrier and get them expressing their feelings. One of the ways I do that is to let the family see me talking to patients about their impending death: 'How do you feel?' 'Any fears?' Frequently they feel relieved to talk about it. They know they're dying, so I make it 'legal' to talk about.

"And when the family really starts talking and sharing with each other, there's a real bonding and healing. And everyone realizes how valuable they are to each other."

Tina adds, "I have a hard time with families and patients who keep from each other that a death is coming. Both need to know. If they don't, it deprives them of comforting each other. And they both know deep down that death is near."

However, teens have a difficult time accepting the reality of dying, according to Mary Fran Hazinki's *Nursing Care for the Critically Ill Child:*

[They] can understand the fact that death is permanent and that it will happen to everyone one day, however ... they fantasize that death may be defied. Adolescents may be unable to totally accept the final reality of death because of belief in their own invincibility.

Because remnants of magical thinking still persist during adolescence, teenagers may view fatal illness as a punishment or may feel guilty. Reassurance and open discussion of feelings, concerns, and fears are extremely important. Adolescents have a great deal of difficulty coping with the idea of their own death at a time when they are striving to establish their own identity and make plans for the future. It is very difficult to face the fact they may have no future.[15]

If you have a friend who is dealing with a terminal illness or chronic condition, talk with him about any feelings of guilt. Remind him that while guilt over sin is real, God's message of SALVATION through faith in Jesus covers all guilt and offers genuine hope, acceptance, and peace. As in all situations, we can "speak the truth in love" (Ephesians 4:15) as we talk with friends and family members about the realities of sin and death and the promises of our loving Father.

Kübler-Ross suggests that adolescents shouldn't be told they are dying, rather they should be told they are "seriously ill."
When they are ready to bring up the issue of death and dying we should answer them; we should listen to them; we should hear the questions, but do not go around telling [teen] patients they are dying and deprive them of a glimpse of hope they may need in order to live until they die.[16]

Do you know when you're dying? How do you know?

Others disagree with Kübler-Ross, pointing out that dying teens already know they're dying—perhaps instinctively because of the increase in medical attention, the way people act toward them, or the tears and awkwardness of visitors.

Regardless, the denial stage is important. It not only helps the medical staff carry on with their other responsibilities, but it gives patients some emotional insulation to make plans and contact family and friends.

Anger

Another phase Kübler-Ross describes is anger, which can come in many forms, among them:

- **Anger at the medical staff:** "Why didn't they detect it earlier?" "Why isn't the medicine working?" "Why wasn't the operation a success?"
- **Anger at God:** "Why did You allow me to get this disease? "Why won't—or don't—You heal me?" One thing my wife does as a professional church worker is tell people it's okay to be angry with God. The psalmists seemed to be angry with God—"Why don't You do something?"—most of the time. (We'll talk more about this in chapter 12.)

This intense anger can spill over onto family and friends. Lynn Caine, in her book, *Widow*, talks about the "craziness" of blaming her husband for dying. How dare he die and "cop out" on his responsibilities to her and their children!

Anger is a **normal emotion** as we deal with our own impending death or the death of a loved one. God created us as emotional beings, and He understands that emotions require expression. It is possible to be angry and not sin—remember the story of Jesus throwing the money changers out of the temple? The patient is losing every earthly thing, and it is understandable that he is angry. Allow him to express it, and don't take it personally.

Bargaining

Family members may pray, "God, if You'll let my grandmother live, I'll go to church more often. I'll even put more in the offering plate. And here's an offer You can't refuse: How 'bout if I become a missionary? You name it, I'll do it."

The patient may pray, "God, just let me make it through the holidays."

Although God bargained with Abraham (Genesis 18) and Hezekiah regarding death (2 Kings 20), God rarely responds to this version of "Let's Make a Deal." It's not that He doesn't care about our hurts and fears. It's that He knows that the best thing He can do is go through life's difficulties with us, not—*poof!*—make all our problems go away.

Depression

It is depressing to think about losses such as health and mobility. In a hospital bed—tethered to an IV pole—you can't play basketball, go out for pizza, swim, walk in the park, or do thousands of things you once enjoyed. The realization creeps in that there may be many more things you'll miss: graduating from high school, going to college, getting married, having children—the list continues to grow in your mind. Kübler-Ross refers to this as **preparatory grief**. The patient and family begin to grieve the loss even before the death.

In chapter 7, we'll talk at length about depression and its symptoms. It's a normal part of the dying process. Although depressed people are depressing to be around, they need our love and company. J. Kerby Anderson, in his excellent book, *Life, Death & Beyond,* writes:

When a patient is expressing himself on an emotional level, he does not need logical arguments. He needs compassion and assurance on the emotional level. Conversely, when he is seeking advice about his personal affairs, he does not need emotional statements like, "Don't worry, everything will be all right." He needs helpful advice about finances or other affairs.[17]

Most important, those facing life-threatening illnesses need to know the truth of God's love in Jesus Christ. Sharing this Good News and focusing on the gifts of forgiveness and *eternal life* that are ours through faith in Jesus bring comfort and hope in the face of death.

Acceptance

Dying patients often come to a point of accepting their impending death with courage and a real lack of fear. They've worked through the denial, anger, bargaining, and depression—often through counseling and support groups. (Organizations such as the American Cancer Society and the Muscular Dystrophy Association sponsor such groups through their local agencies.) Christians find God's healing of their emotions as they spend time reading or hearing His Word—the Bible—or as fellow believers offer their **love and support.**

"Once they reach the acceptance stage," Tina explains, "patients often beg their families to let them go, but the families may put them on 'full code' [order them revived after each heart stoppage]. One patient kept begging her family, 'Don't do this to me. Don't torture me. Let me go!' The family made the doctors and nurses do everything possible to prolong her inevitable death."

Is it scary to know that you're dying?

At this point, the life and death questions of *living wills, death with dignity,* and *euthanasia* (mercy killing) confront the doctors, hospital staff, patients, and families. To further complicate things, the actual **definition** of death continues to change. A few hundred years ago, "lack of breathing" was the evidence of death. This century began by adding "lack of heartbeat" to the criteria. Now "lack of brain wave activity" is a necessary proof.

Tina continues, "Right now the lines are really blurred between passive and active euthanasia. [*Passive euthanasia* is allowing the patient to die without using extraordinary measures. *Active euthanasia* or *assisted suicide* is deliberately causing the patient to die with a lethal injection or some other means.] For instance, we had a man with chronic lung disease who was literally fighting for air for three days. His heart had stopped several times, and each time he had been revived. Finally, he was so 'air hungry' that his physician said, 'We can give you some morphine. It will make you feel better, but it also may cause you to go.' The patient was ready; the family was ready. So he chose morphine, and it wasn't more than 20 minutes and he was gone.

"I'm not sure if that was mercy killing or not. It wasn't a lethal dosage—it was the normal dose for pain control—but it caused him to r e l a x and stop fighting for air. I'm just glad I wasn't the one giving the injection."

Is it okay to pull the plug on someone who's going to die anyway?

Ron adds, "Part of my practice is helping people die, as well as helping people live. I don't put people on medicine I know won't help them. I don't put people on ventilators [who] aren't going to be helped by it.

"I could make an argument for lethal injection. And I can think of cases where it would have been kinder to cut a patient's last days short by a week. I think I could even do it without any problem or real conflict, except—" His voice raises in volume to emphasize the word EXCEPT. "That starts us down a slippery slope that has no ending. Society has slid down that slope with abortions. People now kill millions of unborns that society considers 'unplanned,' an 'inconvenience,' or [a] 'burden on society.' With the rising cost of health care, society is not too far from deciding that the sick and elderly are also a 'burden on society.'"

The Netherlands have already "slid down that slope" with an estimated 5,000 Dutch citizens dying each year with doctors' assistance.[18] America may not be far behind. Marcia Angell, the executive editor of the *New England Journal of Medicine,* writes, "I think perhaps we're ready to consider euthanasia that is very, very strictly controlled."[19]

Dr. Daniel Callahan, one of America's leading bioethicists, writes that on reaching a certain age, the elderly "have no right to burden the public purse." Callahan has suggested that those older than 80–85 be cut off from the "right" to medical care.[20]

Dr. Jack Kevorkian, better known as "Dr. Death," killed nearly 40 people before he was finally convicted by a Michigan court of murder. The main evidence was a videotape Dr. Kevorkian made of this final murder, which TV's *Sixty Minutes* broadcast.

Although there are many factors to be considered in the care of truly terminal patients, both Ron and Tina agree, "When in doubt, choose life."[21]

"With the terminally ill," Ron adds, "I tell them, 'I can't make this go away, but there are two things I can do: I can help keep your pain under control, and I can make sure you're ready to meet God. You can have the peace of knowing that if you die in a month or six months from now, that you will go to heaven. And that's consolation for you and your family.'"

As Ron points out, the best thing you can do for a friend or family member who is dying is love her and share your faith with her. Remind her often that because she believes in Jesus as her Savior, she can be positive of spending eternity with Him.

Dame Cicely Saunders, the founder of the hospice movement, writes, "You matter to the last moment of your life, and we will do all we can, not only to help you die peacefully, but to **live until you die.**"[22]

What's it like when you're on the edge of dying?

Charlene, Tina, and Ron all agree there is a "look" of death. "There's a certain color of the skin," Ron notes. "A pale, whitish blue-gray around the mouth.

There's also fluid build-up in the skin—not in the vessels, but in the tissue—that's a clue that death is near."

Tina adds, "Skin temperature is a clue too. That's why we always check their legs and toes. If they're cold, it means a `lack of circulation.` The body tries to conserve, and so it starts shutting down what it doesn't absolutely need—such as fingers and toes—to conserve blood for the heart and lungs. The fingers and toes feel cold, then turn purple and blue with a 'honeycomb' pattern—blue circles with white in the middle—and then turn completely white. At the very end, the skin gets clammy and then goes beyond clammy to almost wax-like."

A loss of appetite is also a sign of impending death. Well-meaning family and friends will try to force the patient to eat or drink, but dehydration and lack of food actually is a natural way for a dying person to become sleepier and less aware of pain.

A dying person's pulse becomes **weaker** as well. His heart rate begins to drop below what's normal for him. Blood pressure decreases. Breathing becomes shallow. Then his lungs begin filling with fluid, causing a sound some call the "death rattle."

Tina points to one of the monitors. "This patient's QRSs [the space between beats] [are] getting wider, and the peaks are also getting wider. That usually means death is near."

"The patients also become less responsive since there is a loss of blood supply to the brain," Ron adds.

Dying patients often will withdraw and not feel like having visitors. This isn't a sign that they no longer love and care for you, but it is part of the process of breaking ties with the physical world.

"You can pretty well bet if they tell you they're going to die, they probably will,"

Tina continues. "Others will say, 'I don't think I'm going to make it through the night' or 'I'm prepared. I'm going to **meet God.**' They have a sense that death is near—unless it's a sudden death like an accident or sudden stroke."

Charlene has the reputation for being the one on whose shift people die. "A lot of nurses pray, 'God, don't let 'em die on my shift,' but I let them. When they say, 'I'm gonna die,' I don't say, 'You gotta hang in there.' I just hold their hand and say, 'That's okay, I'm here for you. Your family's here for you'—even though most of the family are huddled together in the far corner of the room. Some of the patients are alert to the last minute, and some are unconscious and look like their soul left two days ago and their body hasn't caught up."

Can you know for sure if somebody's dying?

Ron admits, "There's one thing I've learned about working with death, you can't accurately anticipate it. You can have people with all the **symptoms** mentioned and they'll walk out of the hospital a week later. You can have a cancer patient that you expect to live less than six months, and six years later you're still doing their annual examinations. Or, worse, you can tell someone they're perfectly healthy and a few days later they're face-up in a flowerbed from a fatal heart attack.

"So I tell 'terminal' patients, 'You have information that says you're going to die. Perhaps your time period is a little more defined than everybody else's. But you're still in the same situation the rest of us are in. I may well beat you to the grave by walking out the door and getting killed. So it's important to always be ready for death.'" (We'll talk about preparing for death in chapter 11.)

Guilt

Ron adds "guilt" to Kübler-Ross's list of stages. "I see this especially in expectant mothers who lose a baby due to miscarriage or stillbirth. There is a tremendous sense of **guilt** that they somehow caused it—even when it was no fault of their own."

Children may also feel that somehow they contributed to a parent's death. Although this is usually not the case, the feelings are very real.

There is also a temptation for medical personnel to feel guilty with "what ifs." Ron continues, "I look back over the charts to see if I missed anything. The vast majority of the time, if you do find something you missed or could have done differently, it wouldn't have made any difference in the outcome."

Relief

Finally, Ron adds "relief" to the list of stages. "In a terminal illness, there is a tremendous emotional and financial burden for the family and friends. And when the patient dies, there is a sense of relief: 'We can get on with our life.'"

Many survivors feel guilty for feeling relief, but this **emotional release** is healthy and in no way detracts from the value or love they had for the dying person.

Although Charlene, Tina, and Ron have witnessed hundreds of deaths, they admit they still feel the pain. "If I've been close to the person—personally or have been with them professionally for years—I feel the same pain that everyone else does," Ron admits. "And even if there has been very little involvement, it still takes a toll on me like everybody else." (We'll talk about the after-death grieving process in chapter 10.)

Death surrounds the small dispatch room at the Garrett police and fire department.

FBI "Wanted" notices warn of fugitives "armed with automatic weapons, including silencer-equipped machine guns" and who should be considered "heavily armed and dangerous." Angry-looking men with

5 How Can You Deal with Murder?

shaggy hair and three-day-old beards glare out from the **mug shots.**

Beside them, two junior high students—Jacob, 13, and Jaycee, 12—smile from their posters. But the well-moussed hair and good looks hide the fact that they are victims of "stranger abductions." A $20,000 reward is offered for the safe return of Jacob.

On the office TV, *Good Morning America* covers the electric-chair execution of convicted rapist and murderer Roger Keith Coleman. The condemned man, in a taped statement, denies that he raped, stabbed, and nearly beheaded his sister-in-law.

The dispatcher sits surrounded by computers, ash trays, printers, Styrofoam cups of coffee, two-way radios, red telephones, and, of course, the official snack food of law enforcement—a bag of Dunkin' Donuts.

"Custer just pulled up at the side door," the dispatcher announces. "You can meet him there."

As I open the door of the blue Chevy Caprice squad car, the first thing I notice is a 12-gauge shotgun locked upright between Captain Jerry Custer and me. The middle-aged, mustached man wastes no time on chit-chat. "So what do you want to know? Just ask me and I'll give you an **honest** answer. It may not be the answer you want to hear, but I'll give it to you straight."

In less time than it takes the super-charged V-8 engine to pull out of the alley, Jerry has told me that Garrett has a population of 6,500, and that in his 29 years on the force he's personally investigated three murders, four attempted murders, 17 suicides, and too many traffic fatalities to count.

His words shoot out of his mouth with the rapid-fire speed of the Glock .45 automatic strapped to his waist. "It's the meanest, most effective handgun in the world. I use hollow-tipped bullets. They're really safer than smaller caliber bullets that can continue through a wall of an apartment building." He pulls the 13-round clip out of the weapon to show me the bullets. "These things flatten out and stay in whatever you hit. They've got terrific stopping power."

As he steers with one hand and re-holsters his weapon with the other, I have a split second to ask a question. "Any memorable homicides that stand out?"

"Yeah. We're one block from the scene." This time his voice is soft and subdued. He pulls the cruiser up to a run-down gray duplex with gaudy green trim. The porch roof **sags** over boarded-up windows. He now talks slowly and deliberately.

"In 1978 we had the disappearance of a 10-year-old girl named Kaci. She was last seen alive here—had been shoveling snow to make some money to buy a gift for her aunt who had just had a baby."

His voice quivers, then regains its authoritative tone. "I started praying. In fact,

I called my church and told them to start the telephone prayer chain for this little girl. She was in my son's class at school, so I really took it personally." He pauses again. "Because it was winter, we didn't wait the normal 24 hours but got out the dispatch to all the area police departments and news agencies within 12 hours."

"A couple days later, I got a call from the Fort Wayne Fire Department. They had found her hat—a 'Chessie' railroad hat that could only be purchased in Ohio—and her snowmobile boot that also was kinda unique. Soon after that, we found her **body** jammed under a log in Cedar Creek.

"A guy in his 30s had invited her into his apartment and given her some alcohol and some joints. After she had passed out, he stuffed her leotard down her throat and then …" Jerry pauses. "He was a necrophiliac, a guy who has sex with the dead. After he had killed her, he raped her.

"I felt like a big old sheep dog where a wolf had gotten in and got one of the lambs. I felt responsible. There were several times in the investigation that I just went into my office, closed the door, and just **cried**. I just felt so helpless.

"The [jerk] only got seven to 14 years!" His voice rises, and he grips the steering wheel tighter. "I was so ticked off after the trial that I went over to the home of one of the state investigators who had worked the case. We just cried and hugged each other and wondered if there wasn't something we could have done.

"I'm not a 'good cop' because I show my **emotions**. I let stuff get to me—and you just can't, I guess. Sometimes you try to slough it off with humor.

"For instance, you'll go to the scene of a crime that was just discovered—maybe five weeks after the crime. You have to put Vicks VapoRub under your nose just to keep from getting sick from the smell. I remember brushing the flies off a woman's body. When we cut her clothes off to check for foul play, she was covered with maggots.

"Somebody's gotta clean up the mess at a crime scene after everything has been documented by the investigators. But I don't want a mom or a wife to have to clean up a family member's blood and body parts, so I usually say, 'If you've got a mop, I'll clean this up.'

"So as we're sitting at the doughnut shop after cleaning up, we'll be making a lot of jokes about the cream-filled doughnuts looking a lot like what we've just dealt with.

"Another time, I was asked by a woman to come to her house and take the high-powered rifles and compound hunting bows away from her husband who had just gotten out of a mental hospital. I thought, *Great! I get shot with a bow and arrow, and the paper's going to have fun with* 'CUSTER'S LAST STAND.'

"It's not that we joke because we're insensitive—it's just that dark humor helps you keep your sanity sometimes. But a lot of times that doesn't even work. For instance ..." He pulls into a nice residential section of town with cedar-sided apartments set in a grove of pine trees.

"David*—he was 15—lived in apartment 10. He was a good kid, good base-ball player, a hero to a lot of kids. But he got into drugs and dropped out of school. His sister came home from school and there he was, hanging between the living room and dining room.

"My first thought when I got to the scene wasn't, *Is he going to heaven or hell?* It was, ***What a waste!*** Here's a healthy kid who just took his life when other peo-ple, like my dad, were fighting to stay alive with cancer. It just makes me angry."

Jerry pulls out of the apartment parking lot and drives one block to a white-sided house with an attached garage.

*Not his real name

"David's best friend, Matt*—he was 16 at the time—lived here. Matt was a National Honor Society member, and just eight months later, he shot himself through the heart. And then just a few months later, his mom killed herself with carbon monoxide in the garage."

We ride in **silence** for several blocks.

Why do people kill other people?

"What are some of the reasons that people kill others or themselves?" I ask after reflecting on the previous information.

"A lot of the time on reports, we just put down 'personal gain.' That can mean a lot of things: love, lust, revenge. One guy hired a hit man to kill his wife so he wouldn't have to pay alimony after a divorce. The suspect was planning to torch his house to pay the hit man. Fortunately, the 'hit man' was an Indianapolis undercover officer.

"All the **violent crimes** I've investigated—all of 'em—have been drug-related—drugs and alcohol. I see a lot of kids smoking pot, dropping out of school, can't get a job—they get stoned and blow their heads off. One guy who lived there," Jerry says, pointing to a duplex, "was a mental patient who stopped taking his medicine, got suicidal, and put a shotgun under his chin. He

*Not his real name

blew the whole front of his head off. So even that's 'drug related.'

"I'm seeing a lot of what I call 'pagan-related' [deaths]. The media likes to call them 'satanic,' but a lot of them are just impressionable kids looking for meaning in life. I talked to one kid who had a little altar with wax skulls in his bedroom, and he was having this little ceremony and writing the Lord's Prayer backwards. He said, 'I've gotta have something to believe in.'

"Remember David, the kid who hanged himself? On the kitchen table—right by his body—was a book on numerology, a book on astrology, and a Bible opened to the 23rd Psalm. There was also a book called the *Necronomicon*—it's a book of spells that's more popular now than Anton LaVey's *Satanic Bible*. In his bedroom there were also chicken bones and a Ouija board.

"I've also worked attempted suicides where Dungeons and Dragons played a role in the attempt. A lot of people tell me, 'It's just a game like MONOPOLY, but I've never worked any cases where kids attempted suicide playing Monopoly. 'D and D' creates a real fascination with death—and it's dangerous for impressionable young kids.

"And there are some crimes that definitely have 'satanic slaying' clues. There's a gag order on the latest one."

Before the judge ordered all those involved in the case to keep silent, the local newspapers had printed the grisly details of the killing near Garrett. According to the girlfriend of one of the suspects:

Anthony Ault was tied to the floor of a barn ... in Dekalb County. A cross was cut into Ault's body and his neck was slit from ear to ear. When Ault stopped making gurgling noises, his head and hands were cut off and burned in a fire.[23]

Although one of the suspects claims to have been a high priest in a satanic church in Indianapolis, Jerry won't call it a ritualistic killing. "I can tell you this much—the victim knew too much about some other murders, so the **motive** wasn't necessarily a sacrifice to Satan."

"So how do you cope with all these deaths?" I ask.

"There are a lot of times that I'm just driving around and I talk to the Lord. I don't know how I make it some days, but I believe God doesn't give you more than you can handle. I don't wear armor [a bullet-proof vest] all the time—a lot of officers do—but **my armor's God.** Don't get me wrong, if I know I'm going into a hot situation, I'll put it on. But I've never, ever been real fearful in my job."

"Any close calls?" I ask.

"Yeah, right over there." (It seems Jerry has a crime story for every block of the small town.) "I got called out to a domestic dispute—a guy beating … his live-in girlfriend. I pulled up in the squad car to talk with the girlfriend. As we talked on the front porch, I caught movement out of the corner of my eye. The boyfriend had a shotgun aimed out the window and **leveled** right at me.

"All I could do was try to talk him into surrendering the weapon. He had the drop on me, and if I went for my gun, I'd be dead. I finally convinced him that killing me wasn't worth the electric chair, and he dropped the gun.

"Another time I was called to a barroom brawl. I prayed, *God, I'm all alone, and I don't have any backup. Lord, let me know what to do in this situation.* When I came through the door, tables and chairs were tossed around and there were broken bottles all over. I noticed that the one causing all the trouble was a 'good old boy' from down south. It was like God helped me understand that, like most southern boys, he probably had a lot of **respect** for his momma—even if he didn't for me.

"So I walked right up to him and whispered to him, 'I wanna tell you, if I have any trouble with you, I'm gonna tell your momma.' He just walked right out of the bar with me and got in the squad car. People in the bar thought I had some kind of pressure hold on him.

"So I really feel God's help in this work. And I guess it just comes down to doing what you think you ought to be doing. I really feel that I'm one of **God's servants** to the Garrett area."

Stephanie Munson returned to her high school for the first day of school August 16, 1999. That's not unusual except that the school is **Columbine High** in Littleton, Colorado. On April 20, 1999, Eric Harris and Dylan Klebold killed 12 fellow students and a teacher, as well as wounding 23 others, with

How Can You Deal with School Shootings?

semiautomatic weapons and explosives. Stephanie escaped with a gunshot wound to her ankle.

"I remember what happened to me like it was yesterday," the pretty blonde in an Adidas T-shirt says, holding back her emotions. "I have scars everywhere." Going back to school is "just kind of like another scar."

Lance Kirklin's scars are more visible. A deep scar on his left cheek and less noticeable scars on his face and neck reveal how fortunate the 16-year-old was to survive a shotgun blast. His reconstructed mouth doesn't come together perfectly as he says, "You can't change the past. You can only prevail and **move forward.**"

The school's blood-stained carpet has been replaced with white tile. Bullet holes have been patched and walls painted beige. The library, where 10 students were killed and the 18- and 17-year-old killers committed suicide, has been gutted and sealed up with a wall and rows of dark blue lockers.

"I'll never forget what happened, but I'm ready to put it, you know, behind me," Stephanie says.[24]

Some SCARS—especially the ones related to death—God heals slowly, over time.

Why are school shootings so common?

Judging by the 24-hour coverage of Cable News Network (CNN) and the countless "news magazine" TV shows, school shootings are common, everyday

occurrences. Shootings, however, account for only 1 percent of the 5,000 firearms-related deaths of children and young adults under age 19.

And contrary to gun-control advocates, the American Medical Association reports that the number of students packing weapons has steadily declined since 1991. During 1991, 26 percent of 9th-through 12th-grade students reported carrying a weapon in the previous month. The percentage dropped to 22 percent in 1992, to 20 percent in 1995, and to 18 percent in 1997.[25]

Also, the 1996 *Sourcebook of Criminal Justice Statistics* reports that the number of high school students being injured or threatened by someone with a weapon was lower in 1996 than 20 years ago. In 1976, 3.4 percent of seniors were injured by guns compared to 2.8 percent in 1996.[26]

How many [school shootings] are there per day?

While the news coverage of school shootings has increased, the National School Safety Center (NSSC) reports that the number of actual school shootings **decreased** from 55 deaths in 1992–1993 to 25 deaths in 1996–1997![27]

Justice Policy Institute (JPI) Director Vincent Shiraldi believes that school shootings are being used by the media to increase ratings and by gun-control advocates to further their political agendas. "We are witnessing a tragic misdirection of attention and resources … even though the real threat may lie elsewhere."[28]

What can we do to help stop them?

Shiraldi argues that the money spent on surveillance cameras, metal detectors, and armed guards could be better spent on identifying and **counseling** students who show signs of potential violence. As with other school shootings, investigators at Columbine found that "the shooters had made numerous threats or dropped hints that they were contemplating violent action. The perpetrators also had a history of violence or anti-social behavior."[29]

Talk with a school counselor

"Schools want to find these kids and defuse the anger before the time bomb goes off," says Barbara Wheeler, president of the National School Boards Association.[30]

Why do people even think about shooting their classmates?

The U. S. Department of Education's "Guide to Safe Schools" lists several common characteristics of school killers:

- Social withdrawal
- Excessive feelings of rejection
- Being a victim of violence
- Low school interest and poor academic performance
- Expression of violence in writings and drawings directed at specific individuals (family members, peers, other adults)
- Patterns of impulsive and chronic hitting, intimidating, and bullying behaviors
- History of discipline problems
- Past history of violent and aggressive behavior
- Intolerance for differences and prejudicial attitudes
- Affiliation with gangs
- Inappropriate access to, possession of, and use of firearms
- Serious threats of violence[31]

But keep in mind the following warning before calling the authorities about that suspicious classmate in your homeroom:

None of these signs alone is sufficient for predicting aggression and violence. Moreover, it is inappropriate—and potentially harmful—to use the early warning signs as a checklist against which to match indi-

vidual children. **Rather, the early warning signs are offered only as an aid in identifying and referring children who may need help. School communities must ensure that staff and students only use the early warning signs for identification and referral purposes. Only trained professionals should make diagnoses in consultation with the child's parents or guardian.**[32]

Some of the responsibility for a school killer's mental state can be blamed on **fellow students**. Luke Woodham, who killed his mother along with two students in Pearl, Mississippi, told the court, "I'm not insane. I am angry. I killed because people like me are mistreated every day."[33] *Newsweek* quotes classmates of Harris and Klebold as saying they walked the halls of Columbine "with their heads down, because if they looked up they'd get thrown into lockers and get called a 'fag.'"[34] *Time* reports that they were physically threatened and taunted as "dirt bags" and "inbreeds" on a regular basis.[35]

Even some church youth groups and groups of Christian friends are guilty of put-downs, name-calling, and prejudice. Instead of this sinful behavior, Christians are free to love one another—even our enemies—as God has loved us. God's love caused Him to send His Son, Jesus, to earth to associate with the "wrong crowd" and earn forgiveness for all sinners. God wants us to share His AWESOME LOVE with *everyone* around us, not just other Christians or those in our own circle of friends.

Peer influence is only part of the picture in school violence. Another factor is the number of guns and the apparent ease with which kids can lay their hands on guns. Violent video games and movies also have been blamed for killings in schools. Other experts claim the school systems themselves share some responsibility for the killings in their halls. These critics point out that when students are taught that they've evolved from **pond scum** and that there are no moral absolutes, administrators may not be able to expect students to treat one another better than pond scum or to understand the difference between right or wrong.

While all this finger pointing doesn't excuse the murderers, it may help explain, in part, what motivated the killings.

The Department of Education's "Guide to Safe Schools" also lists "imminent warning signs" that indicate that "a student is very close to behaving in a way that is potentially dangerous to self and/or to others." These signs are

- Serious physical fighting with peers or family members
- Severe destruction of property
- Severe rage for seemingly minor reasons
- Detailed threats of lethal violence
- Possession and/or use of firearms and other weapons

- Other self-injurious behaviors or threats of suicide[36]

If you are aware of a student exhibiting these symptoms, **immediately** contact your school principal. (Some schools have set up special hotlines so you can confidentially report these kinds of behaviors.)

It comes down to this: School shootings actually are very **rare**. The media play up the sensational killings for increased ratings and the anti-gun political groups use the abuse of weapons to further their agendas. You may want to compare the situation to tornadoes or hurricanes. Deaths caused by these storms are very rare, but the home videos of nature's wrath, along with reporters standing beside rubble that once was a quiet neighborhood, make great television news. However, as long as we take the warnings seriously, there is little danger of death.

Remember, you're more likely to be struck by lightning than to be killed at school. But do take **storm warnings** seriously.

"I can't do anything with my hair!" Judy heard Terri, her 16-year-old daughter, complain Monday morning.

"Maybe you could get a perm over spring break, honey. Dad's already left for work and I'm running late, so have a good day at school," Judy said as she gave her daughter a quick kiss on the cheek

How Can You Deal with Suicide?

and hurried from the house. "Oh, your lunch money is on the kitchen counter."

When Judy returned home that afternoon at 5 o'clock, Terri's school bag and lunch money were still on the counter. Before she had time to **wonder** where her daughter was, the phone rang.

"Hi, Mrs. Davis. This is Steve. Is Terri there?"

"No, maybe she's out running. It's such a beautiful spring day." But a quick glance around the family room revealed that Terri's running shoes were exactly where she had kicked them off the night before.

"Oh, I was just wondering since she wasn't in school today."

Judy's heart began to **pound** as she hung up the phone and rushed to her daughter's room. Terri's nightshirt was tossed on the bed, but the clothes she had picked out for school were there too.

"Charlie," Judy nearly shouted to her husband when he answered her phone call to him. "Terri's missing."

Charlie, too, began to panic. "It's not like Terri to not leave a note if she's going to be gone."

When Charlie pulled into the driveway, he noticed that their third car, "The Bomb," was missing. As Charlie walked toward the front door, he glanced into the garage. There was "The Bomb" with all the **dash lights** on.

Judy noticed Charlie's frightened expression. "Stay here, Judy. I think I found Terri."

As he opened the garage door, Charlie was nearly overcome by the exhaust fumes. There, in the backseat, slumped over, was Terri. Charlie pounded on the top of the car and screamed, "Oh my God, no! No!"

"When I touched her, she was cold and hard. I knew she had been dead for a long time," her father recalls as we sit talking with a tape recorder and a plate of chocolate chip cookies between us.

"This is a picture of Terri." Charlie proudly, tenderly takes a photo down from the wall. Judy and Charlie Davis speak about the **suicide** of their daughter with determined, controlled emotions. During the five years since Terri's death, they have spoken at numerous high schools—including Terri's own school—about the growing problem of teen suicide.

How many teens commit suicide?

More than 5,000 young people between the ages of 15 and 24 kill themselves each year. That same number **attempt** suicide every *day*.[37]

Down Times Are Normal

Judy takes a sip of coffee and a deep breath. "We just thought Terri was going through the normal ups and downs that typical teens go through."

Charlie agrees. "Looking back, we can see the symptoms of depression, but at the time—and even now—it didn't seem to be more than the normal stress of adolescence."

What's the most common reason for suicide?

In the first book of this series, *When Can I Start Dating?*, I spend several chapters assuring teens that adolescent changes are "normal, healthy, and temp rary." Times of depression are a part of that hormone-driven **roller**

coaster. Even saints such as Moses, Elijah, and Jonah went through periods of extreme depression and, yes, suicidal thoughts! (Check out Numbers 11:10–15; 1 Kings 19:1–5; and Jonah 4:9.) But keep in mind that

Down Times Are Temp-orary

Judy warns teens that "death is so final. If you take your life, you'll never go to your junior-senior prom, you're never going to go to college, you're never going to see your friends get married. That's it. There's no coming back. So I tell students, 'Try to make it through the next week, or the next day, or even the next hour.'"

If you're thinking about suicide, consider this: Suicide is a permanent solution to a temporary problem. No matter how bad you may feel now, it's probably only temporary. Most times of depression last only a few hours or days. Very few last a month or more. Be encouraged that if you get some outside help, feelings of depression don't have to be permanent.

You will, without a doubt, have high days and low days in your life. But mostly there will be ordinary days. You know, the ones where you just go through the motions of school, home, or church. They're not bad days, but they're nothing to write your e-mail "buddy list" about, either.

There are even "low days" on the calendar. Most suicides occur on Monday. There are other days that we are prone to depression: the week before school finals, term paper deadlines, the first or last day of classes (depending on if you love or hate school). February 14 can be a low day if you don't have a valentine or a date for the big school party. Anniversaries of a loss or tragedy can bring low days back each year, often in living color and stereo sound.

There are also certain times of year when suicides happen more often. November has the most suicides of any month. It looks depressing when the days are growing colder and nights are growing longer. Upcoming holidays often emphasize family problems or breakups. (You won't be together or you won't be looking for a present for that special person this year.)

Even a girl's monthly "cycle," sickness, high and low air pressure, seasons of the year, or, yes, eating pepperoni pizza before bed can affect your mood.

But there is hope!

Down Times Can Be Overcome

The prophet Isaiah had some down times too. He wrote:

[God] gives strength to the weary and increases the power of the weak. Even youths grow tired and weary, and young men stumble and fall; but those who hope in the LORD will renew their strength. They will soar on wings like eagles; they will run and not grow weary, they will walk and not be faint. (Isaiah 40:29-31)

Down times (even occasional thoughts of ending it all) are normal ingredients in life. It may take some time to get over the feelings of hurt and disappointment, and that's tough because we live in an "instant" society. We're used to instant drinks, microwave popcorn, and fast food. Sometimes we think our emotional state should change in 30 seconds or less. "Just add a little alcohol or drugs to taste," our friends may suggest. Even some churches offer instant recipes: Just pray about it and all your problems will instantly disappear. But none of these instant cures work.

It's true that the only one who can help us endure and

overcome bad times is God. He is powerful and able. But He isn't a vending machine or a magic wand that will just make it better. He is there to go through our low times with us, not to make the low times disappear. Those who trust in Him discover a **HOPE** humans can't create on their own.

Down Times May Be a Sign of Physical Exhaustion

The cure for down times or depression may be as simple as getting caught up on sleep! Here's part of a letter from a teen named Brad:

Last year, I was really hopping to keep up. I had a full schedule of accelerated courses. I was in the choir, in the school play, had a paper route, was the youth group treasurer, and was trying to keep honor-roll grades.

About January, I was physically and emotionally wiped out. I couldn't have cared less about anything. I just sat there like a zombie. I got nothing. I gave nothing. I was getting depressed.

I finally told our youth sponsor about my schedule. She said I didn't need to go to a doctor or the minister. I just needed to go to bed.

Anyway, to make a long story short, I got out of several of those things and began to get more sleep each night. What a difference!

In a month's time, I bounced back and was full of joy that I hadn't felt for so long.

Down Times May Be a Sign of Spiritual Emptiness

Sometimes what we call depression is actually the emptiness we feel when God is left out of our lives. It's important to note that everyone experiences some difficulty or discouragement, but life with Christ can be filled with internal joy, love, peace, and hope. You may want to skip ahead to chapter 18 to read how God wants to help in this area of your life. You may be amazed what a difference He will make!

And remember, there is nothing—absolutely nothing—you've done that God won't forgive if you ask Him!

Fifteen-year-old Matt* forgot that. Here are two actual letters he wrote to his high school and to his brother.

*Not his real name.

PLEASE READ THE FOLLOWING TO THE HIGH SCHOOL KIDS!!

Now everything is a big joke. Parties, Drugs, Booze and fun. Well stop and look where you are going. I laughed at the warnings too and now look where I'm at. Dead!!! You that heard me preach saw how God changed my life. He can change yours too!! When he does, You better not turn back. Discipline yourselves now!! Draw near to God through Jesus Christ now!!! If you don't begin practicing obedience and self-discipline now, you may some day find yourselves hopeless. It's your choice. Everyone of you who are messing with Drugs can see how it's affecting your true care and love for anyone but yourselves. For your own sakes. Stop now before it's too late. Jesus Christ cares about YOU! He wants YOU to choose Him. Don't forsake him. Draw close to Him and OBEY him.

Dear Michael,

Don't rebel against your teachers and elders Michael. Work hard in school now. If your friends think you are a chicken if you don't misbehave don't worry about it. STAY AWAY FROM DRUGS AND ALL THOSE E.S.P. AND OTHER THINGS YOU ARE MESSING IN. REMEMBER THE THINGS I SPOKE TO YOU ABOUT WHEN I WALKED CLOSE TO GOD. REMEMBER HOW I CHANGED. God can change you too Michael. He can give you the peace you didn't have at home. Get close to Him and STAY THERE!! Discipline your mind while your still in school. Don't run wild like all the other kids.

GOD FORGIVE ME FOR NEGLECTING YOU AND FOR BECOMING SO COLD!! TAKE CARE OF MICHAEL AND MOM. HAVE MERCY ON MY SOUL. AMEN.

After finishing these two letters, Matt shoved the barrel of a .22 rifle in his mouth and pulled the trigger. Don't make Matt's mistake. There is help—and **FORGIVENESS** for Christ's sake—available to you and your friends. Faith in God does give your life meaning.

How can you stop someone from committing suicide?

First, be aware of the following warning signs that the problem is greater than the normal ups and downs of life.

- Going through mood swings.
- Showing signs of depression. These signs include lack of concentration; deep-rooted boredom; withdrawal; eating too much or too little; lack of energy; self-criticism; negative thinking; feelings of guilt, shame, fear, or helplessness; rebellion; over-confidence; lack of fear of injury or death.
- Having problems at school.
- Having problems communicating.
- Displaying any sudden change in behavior. A sudden improvement in attitude may mean the individual has made the decision to commit suicide and now feels a sense of relief or control.
- Increasing the use of alcohol or drugs.
- Giving away personal property.
- Displaying self-destructive behavior.
- Talking about suicide, particularly the specifics of how it will be done.

Second, know what to do if someone close to you talks about suicide.

- Always take talk about suicide seriously. Never say, "You're not really going to kill yourself" or "You don't have the guts to do that." Assume your friend means exactly what he or she is saying.

- Pray that God will help you stay calm and compassionate.

- Assure your friend of your concern and God's love for him or her, even if that person has disobeyed Him.

- Assure your friend that feelings of depression are natural and can be overcome with proper help. Try to convince him or her that suicide is a permanent "solution" for a temporary problem.

- Don't promise to keep secrets about suicidal talk or attempts if your friend won't seek help on his or her own.

- Offer to go with him or her to talk to a professional.

Third, know what to do if your friend makes specific plans to commit suicide.

- Tell your friend you are not going to leave him or her alone and you are calling for help; then do it! Call 911, the police, a suicide hotline, the mental health clinic, or your pastor or youth worker. Don't leave the person alone until professional help arrives.

- Again, don't try to handle the situation by yourself. And don't put yourself in any unnecessary danger.

If you have had long-lasting feelings of depression or thoughts of suicide, you need to talk to a professional. Your **first stop** should be your family doctor. He or she can help you find out if there is a physical cause for your depression. Researchers have discovered that chemical imbalance in the brain often is the cause of clinical depression. Prescription drugs often easily correct the problem. It's no more a disgrace to take antidepressant drugs than to take insulin or allergy medicine. Part of God's care for us includes medical options such as antidepressant medications, which can correct bodily imperfections.

If you need emotional help, your pastor, youth director, parents, or school counselor may be able to help you. If they can't, they will refer you to others who can. Always remember: There is hope!

Remember, too, that down times are normal, they're temporary, and they can be overcome with the right help. You don't ever have to feel that you are totally defeated. Believe it![38]

If, tragically, a friend of yours or someone you know does end his or her life, it's easy to feel that you somehow let that person down or could have done more to keep him or her from committing suicide. Judy and Charlie agonized

over what they could have done to avert Terri's death. Such feelings of responsibility are normal but seldom true.

Can a Christian commit suicide and still go to heaven?

Suicide is a personal choice made by the person who commits it. Only that person is ultimately responsible for his or her actions—but is this true? Many health-care professionals believe that suicide is an irrational act—a type of "temporary insanity."

If this is truly the case, then the haunting question "Will a

Christian who commits suicide still go to heaven?" may be answered. As we'll discuss later in chapter 18, we don't go to heaven because of our "good deeds" or go to hell because of our "bad actions." The Bible tells us that faith in Jesus as our Savior is the work of the Holy Spirit (1 Corinthians 2:14; Ephesians 2:8–9). However, God created human beings with free will, which means people can exercise their ability to reject this gift. In effect, they tell God they don't need Him, Jesus, or His forgiveness or eternal life.

We don't know what's going on inside another person's heart, especially when it comes to his or her belief and trust in God. Only God knows whether someone who commits suicide is rejecting God or merely behaving in an irrational manner. So it's difficult to answer whether a Christian who commits suicide will go to heaven. What we do know is that, for Jesus' sake, God will judge each of us in mercy and grace.

"You're here to do what?!" the receptionist at The Stone and Stone Chapel stammers.

"I'm here to watch an EMBALMING. Mike made the arrangements," I answer.

"What do you want to do that for?" the woman questions as she stares sideways at me. I can almost

How Can You Deal with Dead Bodies?

hear the sound of her suspicious brain cells: *Is this guy crazy? ... an inspector with the Indiana State Board of Health? ... a serial killer?*

"I'm writing a book about death," I say to try to reassure her.

"Oh. I never go back to the prep room." She shakes her head, shrugs her shoulders, then goes back to reading the morning paper.

Mike Stone is not a stereotypical "undertaker." He's 28 and dressed like a young urban professional. "Hi, Jim. I'm just beginning to prepare a body, so come right on back."

Mike leads me to a door with a sign that warns:

"Danger: Health Risk. Employees Only Past This Point." Before opening it, he explains, "We have two bodies in the preparation room today. One is a 70-year-old woman who has been prepared, dressed, and placed in her casket. The second one, which I'll be working on today, is an 80-year-old woman who just died last night."

As Mike opens the door, my eyes focus first on the casket with the 70-year-old. The colored floodlights above it give the skin the typically pink glow I'm familiar with. Then, out of the corner of my eye, I see a completely naked body lying on a stainless steel table. There is nothing pink or glowing about her yellowish-white skin and white hair.

"Here's a lab coat and an apron," Mike offers. He puts on thick latex gloves—more like cleaning gloves than surgical gloves—and plastic goggles.

What's embalming like?

I feel uncomfortable looking at the body. It's certainly not sexually arousing, but I feel like I'm invading the woman's privacy. I maintain eye contact with Mike instead.

"Are these precautions against AIDS?" I ask.

"Well, actually we're more worried about hepatitis. It's a viral infection of the liver and is transmitted by blood. You can usually tell someone who's died of HIV. They'll be really thin. But you or I could have hepatitis right now and not know it, so we presume that every body is carrying some dangerous disease. Usually the hospital or health-care facility will put an orange or green tag on the toe that says 'Take Extra Precautions with Body Fluids.' The goggles are for the **formaldehyde**. You can go blind if you get it in your eyes."

Do you mess your pants when you die?

Mike picks up a spray bottle—the kind glass cleaner comes in—and begins to spray the body from face to feet. "First, we thoroughly disinfect the body and wipe out any fluids in the mouth, eyes, nose, genitals, and rectum with cotton. When a person dies, all the **muscles relax**, so most release the contents of their bladder at death."

The table has a one-inch lip around it, and water continually flows from a hose at the head to a drain at the feet.

"The legal definition of *embalming* is 'disinfection, preservation, and restoration.' Restoration means making the body look more **lifelike**," Mike explains.

"After we've thoroughly washed the body, we begin 'setting features' or positioning the body as it will look in the casket."

Mike pulls what looks like a staple gun out of a drawer. "This is a needle injector," he explains as he opens the body's mouth. I force myself to watch. He pulls her upper lip back toward her nose, exposing her gums. They, too, are as white as the rest of her body. With a metallic *click* and a muffled *thud*, the gun drives a barbed needle with a piece of wire trailing off the end into her top gum. He pulls down the lower lip and fires a second needle and wire into the lower gum. "Now, we pull the jaws firmly closed and twist these wires together. At the time of death, muscles go limp and this will keep the mouth from opening."

Do they really sew your eyes shut?

Next, he takes "eye caps," which look like large contact lenses, and smears them with industrial strength petroleum jelly. He carefully pries open each eye, positions the plastic disc on the eyeball, then closes each eye. "This keeps the eyes closed and keeps them moist so they don't dehydrate and disfigure. I've been to some funeral homes where they haven't done this procedure and the eyes popped open."

"Next we want to 'raise vessels.' If a person has lost a lot of weight, we want to 'puff up' the body with embalming fluid." Mike takes a scalpel and makes a two-inch cut just above where the right leg connects to the body. I'm surprised at the lack of blood and lack of color in the tissues as Mike cuts through skin and muscle.

"Most of the blood has settled into the low spots at the back of the body," Mike explains. "I'm looking—actually feeling—for the femoral artery." He speaks with authority and yet a casual ease, as if he's teaching a **biology class** how to dissect a fetal pig. Fortunately, I enjoyed dissecting in high school and college, so I keep telling myself this is just a larger assignment. I try not to think of this "body" as a grandmother or great-aunt.

"Arteries are pearl-colored, but the veins running right beside them are gorged with blood. I'm going to tie a piece of surgery string around the artery." I'm amazed at how delicately his fingers work through the thick rubber gloves.

"Next, we'll make an incision just above the collar bone on the right side to find the jugular vein. We'll inject through the artery and drain through the vein." Again, there's no blood as he quickly locates the vein, which is dark blue, and ties surgical string around it.

"We'll use chemicals to dissolve the coagulated—or gelled—blood. The longer [the time] between death and embalming, the harder it is to embalm."

Mike turns to the Duo-Tronic II embalming pump. A five-gallon glass container sits on metal housing with pressure gauge dials and switches for "Low/High" and "Pulsate." The sign above it warns: "DANGER. Formaldehyde. Irritant and Potential Cancer Hazard. Personnel Only."

Mike adds about one gallon of water to the tank. "Next we'll add PH-A, which helps break up blood clots and then DI-CEN, which is a co-injection. DI-CEN promotes formaldehyde penetration into the tissue. It also treats the water to make it the same pH factor as the body.

"I'm using HY-FORM, which is formaldehyde with the highest index or strength. The higher the index, the higher [the] degree of 'fixative.' The more fixative, the more rigid it makes the skin. The lower the index, the softer and more lifelike the flesh will feel. I'm using the highest index because she's 80 years old and probably has some clogged arteries. I want to get the most preserving action possible on the first try.

"Next, I'll add some red coloring to give more natural flesh tones. Now, while that's mixing, we'll open the artery."

Mike makes a small incision in the wall of the artery. "This is a *cannula*," he explains. It looks like a thick hypodermic needle with an air pump connector on the end. He inserts it into the artery, then ties it in place with more surgical thread. Mike then connects the hose from the pump to the cannula in the artery.

"The embalming machine can force fluid into the body up to 30 pounds per square inch. We'll set it on five pounds today. The machine can also pulsate to circulate the fluid just as the heart would have.

"Normally, I'd open the vein now, but I want to 'puff up' the body since she's lost a lot of weight. The fluid expands the tissue, then sets up." Mike points to the veins on the woman's head. "See the veins on her temple rise," he says almost reverently. The pulsating action of the machine makes the body seem alive for the first time. A lifelike pink glow begins to spread across her face and down her left side as we both watch with a sense of awe.

After a gallon of fluid has been pumped into the body, Mike opens the jugular vein on the side of the neck to relieve the pressure. He inserts a drain tube, which looks like a long, thin kitchen whisk, into the vein. "Since she's been dead for eight hours, the blood has begun to clot, so this will break up any large clots. Sometimes you have to press on the chest to create some internal pressure to force the clots out." Mike thrusts the tube in and out of the vein. Suddenly, a gush of thick, curdled blood gushes out of the vein. The red river flows over her shoulder and cascades onto the table.

"Uh, do you have a bar stool I could sit on?" I try to ask casually as, suddenly, I feel hot, out of breath, and weak in the knees. As Mike goes to get a chair, I realize this is not a science project. The *lub-dub, lub-dub* of the machine sounds like a heart as the yellowish-white skin continues to turn to a lifelike pink. This is—or I should say *was*—somebody's sister, wife, mother, grandmother, or aunt.

Mike returns. I eagerly sit down and try to control my emotions. "How did you feel when you prepared your first body?" (I'm hoping he felt this squeamish as well!)

"I've grown up in the business. As a little boy, I watched my dad do this—it wasn't something gross, just something you have to do. I worked in here as much as I could in high school, so it was second nature. The funeral service is family oriented. There are a lot of second- and third-generation funeral homes. It's just like if your grandfather and your father ran a hardware store—you're more than likely to carry on the

family business.

"So it's no different than shelving bolts and tools at the hardware store. And sometimes it can be almost that impersonal. Here's a body without any clothes on. We're cutting into them—obviously with no anesthetic. You can lose the sense of personality. Not that we're disrespectful in any way, but it's just another body that needs to be embalmed.

"But it's really tough if it's a friend or associate in the community. Three of my friends from my high school class had been drinking and were hit by a train and were killed. The mother of one of them called me and said, 'I want you to take care of my son.' That was really hard. There were times I was sweating, as white as a sheet, and had to leave and get some air.

"So if you know them, it can be very emotional for the funeral director as well. My father and I worked on Grandma and Grandpa. People asked us, 'Wouldn't you want someone else to do it?'" (I was about to ask that question!) Mike continues. "Our answer was no. I wouldn't want anyone else to do it. It's something that I can do that nobody else can do. You want to take care of your family, so it's kinda like a **tribute** to them.

"To be a sensitive funeral director, my dad says you must have a death in your own family once every six months. I've seen some funeral homes where you're just another number. So you have to watch out that you don't get caught up in just the mechanics. We have three funerals tomorrow, so we have to make sure schedules are worked out, vehicles are ready, and so on. But when someone calls with a loved one who just died, that's more important to them than schedules—it's probably the most traumatic thing that's ever happened to them.

"And there's an advantage in knowing the person. You know their features, their skin color, how they smile. People show emotions through their eyes, but when they're dead, it has to be through their mouth." Mike pushes up the corners of the woman's mouth. "So we try to work a bit of a smile into the face—to show a little emotion." He keeps working with the mouth. "The embalming fluid remains liquid, but the tissue begins to fixate, so you keep working to get just the right position of the body."

Why do people get stiff when they die?

"When does **rigor mortis** set in?" I ask.

"From about eight hours to 16 hours. After death, the cells continue to produce energy. When they begin to die, they begin setting up. The stiffness peaks at about eight hours and then loosens up after another eight hours. So if you pick up a body and it's limp and loose, you can guess that the person's been dead for at least 16 hours."

What does a dead body feel like?

I finally work up enough nerve to touch the body. The skin feels like an orange skin that has been left out at room temperature. After watching the body's blood drained and poisonous chemicals pumped in, there's no question that there's no life left in this body.

"We want to make them look l i f e l i k e¬" Mike says as he pulls out a hypodermic syringe and draws some fluid out of the tank. "See how the fingertips are wrinkled and shriveled up—kinda like when you get out of the tub?" He inserts the needle in the fingertip and injects fluid as the fingertips slowly begin to swell and look soft and wrinkle-free. "It's just one of the tricks of the trade to make the body look more lifelike."

He turns the woman's hand over to reveal ugly purple and black splotches on the back of her hand. "Those are bruises from IV treatments," he explains. "We'll inject some Dryene between the skin and the flesh and that will bleach those marks out. It also burns off any blood vessels that would continue leaking under the skin."

Although Mike's schedule is full today, he takes extra time to make seven more incisions to try to embalm parts of her body that have been cut off with blood clots. "Sometimes you can get a good embalming with just the groin incision and can use only the femoral artery and vein. Unfortunately, we can't [do that] in the very elderly."

After Mike is fully convinced that the fluid has reached every part of the body, he begins tying off all the arteries and veins he has cut. He then pours incision sealer into the cuts. The fine white powder hardens into a plaster-like sealant whenever it comes in contact with fluids.

"I then stitch up the incisions with what's called a baseball stitch," Mike explains as he sews back and forth in a pattern that does look exactly like the stitching on a baseball.

"What do you call the S-shaped needle, Mike?" I ask.

"An *S-shaped needle*. Here, would you like to do some stitching?"

"Uh, I don't think so," I quickly reply. "Now, are you finished?"

"No. After the body has set for several hours—to allow the fluids to work—we do what's called *aspiration*. The embalming fluid has preserved the actual tissue and the outside of the heart and organs, but we've not dealt with anything on the inside where germs and bacteria are still living in the dead body. There's a lot of blood still in the heart, food in the stomach, and fecal matter in the intestines, so we use this …"

Mike unveils a 22-inch hollow tube with a pointed end and three holes just above the point. "This is called a *trocar*," he announces, grasping the handle grip on the end of the chrome-plated instrument. "We go up two inches from the navel and insert this into the body cavity and try to hit every major organ. The aspirator— which is a special vacuum pump—connects on this end and sucks out blood, food, feces, urine, and other body fluids. Then we'll fill the cavity with 32 ounces of high-concentration formaldehyde." (I'm grateful that I'm not a witness to aspirating.)

Finally, Mike bathes the body from head to toe with disinfectant soap, washes down the table, then shampoos the woman's hair with Rave Moisturizing Shampoo, which promises to "Restore Moisture to Dry Hair." He combs out her hair, then applies Kalon Cosmetic Massage Cream to the face and hands. "It helps keep the moisture in," Mike explains. "Tomorrow her beautician will come and fix her hair and make her up," Mike notes as he **respectfully** covers the body with a pink sheet, leaving the head uncovered.

Do you have to be embalmed?

"Is embalming mandatory?" I ask.

"Not in Indiana. But our policy here is 'no embalming, no public viewing.' Without embalming, a dead body can be deadly to those coming in contact with it. One woman committed suicide and wasn't found for three days—in a very warm room—so she was in advanced stages of decomposition. It was so bad that when you touched her skin, it fell off. So you certainly don't want to expose families to that kind of sight—or smell—without embalming.

"And then there are some bodies that are so badly injured or decomposed that you can't embalm them. You can only put them in a plastic body bag and seal it up."

Mike turns to clean his instruments in the sink, then lays them in a tray of disinfectant. He carefully washes his gloves before removing them. "Working here, you're reminded of your own MORTALITY every day. Maybe I see that more than other people my age. Most of my friends are thinking about careers and advancement—the last thing they think about is death. But I deal with it every day.

"How can people work in this business and not be Christians?" Mike asks staring at the body on the table. "And how can people stand at a casket with no hope of **eternal life**? You ask a lot of questions in this business." (We'll talk about some of those questions in the next chapter.)

Part THREE

How Are You Supposed to React to Death?

The best thing to say to someone who has just lost a loved one is …

That's right! Often the best thing to say is **nothing**—a shared tear, a squeezed hand, a hug, or just being there during this time of grief is often the most helpful thing to do.

9 What Do You Say at a Funeral?

Jim Stone, who has been a funeral director for more than 30 years, admits he still doesn't have pat answers for the plea, "I'm hurting and I don't know what to do."

"I usually tell people in the mourning process, 'Say what your heart tells you to say. That's pretty safe. Most of all, don't have a prepared speech. Be sensitive enough to go with the flow and say whatever you feel is needed at the time.'

"Many times, teens are looking for clues for what to say or do, so each funeral has a different emotional response. For instance, hysteria feeds hysteria, and so we may have a very emotional service. Not that the teens are disrespectful in any way, but there is a lot of outward expression—crying and touching the deceased. I've even seen people kiss the body on the forehead or mouth. You won't catch me doing that, but I don't discourage it. At other times, there are just as strong emotions, but it's very quiet and subdued.

"Although teens don't always know how to act or how to express themselves at a funeral, I've never seen any joking or laughing or a party attitude. They've always been very respectful because death is a very **sobering** thing.

"But, again, if you follow what your heart is telling you, you're usually safe."

What shouldn't you say at a funeral?

There are some things that you *shouldn't* say, Jim advises.

Never say, "Passed away"

No one seems to "die" in our culture. They've simply been **called home**, given up the ghost, returned to dust, gone the way of all mortal flesh, flown to their heavenly reward, crossed over the Jordan, traveled on to glory, moved upstairs to sing in the heavenly choir.

Less religious people may use phrases such as on ice, six feet under, pushing up daisies, or shoveling coal. Their meter has expired. They've breathed their last, met the Grim Reaper, keeled over, bit the big one, kicked the bucket, **bought the farm**, cashed in their chips, closed up shop, made the final deadline, went home feet first, shuffled off to Buffalo, or brought down the final curtain. The fat lady has sung; Elvis has left the building.

Actually, they're D-E-A-D!

Jim Stone continues, "One of the most important reasons for a funeral is to help the family and friends realize that their loved one has 'died.' Christians do have the hope that the one they love 'has gone to his eternal reward,' but as a funeral director, I must help them cope with the fact that the **earthly** relationship is over.

"Friends and family can help overcome this natural denial mechanism by using the words *died* or *death*. This isn't always easy, but it is very necessary in the process of completing the earthly relationship. We're not being honest—psychologically or spiritually—to try to lessen what has occurred by avoiding the 'D-word.'"

As we'll learn in the next chapter, the first step in dealing with grief is to admit that there is something to grieve about.

Never say, "I understand; I know how you feel."

Even if you've experienced an identical loss—such as you've both lost a grandparent—there are many things that you don't "understand" or "know." What kind of relationship did your friend have with his grandparent? Maybe the two were quite close or maybe they only saw each other at Christmastime. What were the last words spoken? Were they loving or harsh? What kinds of questions, thoughts, and feelings are churning in your friend's mind? What is your friend's belief about life after death?

You really can't know **exactly** what another person is feeling. But you can be a source of real healing in the mourning process by saying how you felt: "When my grandmother died, I felt like …" then tell him. In this way, you're letting your friend know you've experienced a similar loss and are allowing him the freedom to tell you how he feels.

Is it okay to cry out loud at a funeral?

Never say, "Don't cry; be strong."

Your friend is already struggling with overwhelming feelings. (We'll talk about such feelings in the next chapter.) You don't need to make him feel that he's weak, immature, or not handling the death well by adding shame and guilt to his emotional load. Allow your friend to express how he feels.

Jim Stone adds, "I've noticed that guys today are much more open to expressing their emotions. I see that as a healthy sign."

On the other hand, be careful not to make your friend feel guilty for not showing outward emotion. He may still be in the shock or denial stage that we'll talk about in the next chapter. Or he may just be a guy! Western culture has taught males that "big boys don't cry," but there may be a biological reason as well. Males actually have less of the hormone prolactin that is needed to produce tears. The emotional pain may be just as intense for males as for females, but biology and culture make it difficult for guys to show it.

Should you talk about how somebody died?

Never say, "You don't have to talk about the details of the death."

We often think that by asking a survivor about the details of the death, we'll cause more pain and sorrow. So we carefully avoid words such as *cancer, suicide, drowning, shooting,* or *AIDS.*

Surprisingly, most survivors *want* to talk about how their loved one died. My wife's mother must have told the story of how her husband died at least 10 times while the family was gathered at her home during the days before the funeral. But each time she told the story—how he said she'd better call the ambulance, how he collapsed on the dining room floor and cut his forehead on the telephone stand, how she tried to initiate CPR like she had seen on TV—she seemed to gain emotional strength and comfort.

Talking about the details also helps move survivors past the denial stage and into the mourning process.

Never quote Scripture or sentimental clichés

Scripture warns, "Like one who takes away a garment on a cold day, or like vinegar poured on soda, is one who sings songs to a heavy heart" (Proverbs 25:20). For instance, while delivering our daughter, my wife, Lois, vomited from the anesthetic and breathed the fluid into her lungs. It's called *asporadic pneumonia,* and the last three women at St. Mary's Hospital with the condition had died within hours.

So I sat in the Intensive Care Unit for five days, not sure if Faith would have a mother or if I would still have a wife. People who came to visit me were very kind, but they would simply stop by long enough to quote a Bible verse, then leave me alone to sit for several more **agonizing** hours.

My undergraduate work was in theology, so I *knew* all the verses—and I resented the "hit and run" sermons. I wasn't ready for answers at that point. I needed someone to sit with me in that LONELY waiting room. Fortunately, Peggy Ogg came by with an Uno deck and spent one afternoon playing cards with me. That was more helpful than all the Bible verses because I needed someone to be *with* me, not talk *at* me.

Please, don't misunderstand me. I have the utmost respect for God's Word. But often, people in the initial stages of grief need our ears more than our mouths. And sometimes they just need our warm body in the same cold room—and nothing more. Most important, simply express your love for them. As you express your love, you are sharing God's love with them. Then wait for them to tell you what they want to talk about.

A 15-year-old wrote on the survey:

I feel sad. My grandmother died three years ago. I live right next to her house. Now my aunt lives in it. I spent my childhood at her house with my cousins. Every time I go in, I want to cry. I'm not sure what to do. I got her dog, Taffy, when she died. After she died, Taffy

When Does It Stop Hurting?

would go down to the house and wait on the porch for Grandma to let her in.

I'm not sure if there is life after death. All I know is that I miss my grandmother. I never even got to say good-bye. She died in the afternoon. When I came home from school, I went to her house. She wasn't there. My uncle told me she was in the hospital, but he didn't tell me that she had died. My mom and my sister and I didn't find out until about 8:00 that night that she had died.

How can I tell her good-bye and that I love and miss her?

Can you feel this young woman's pain of loss? That's what GRIEF is—an emotion of loss. Perhaps you have felt it when a parent moved away after a divorce, when you broke up with a boyfriend or girlfriend, or when you moved away from your old neighborhood. Even losing a valued object (such as a class ring) or an important ball game creates a sense of grief. There's a feeling of separation and loss.

Why do you hurt when someone you love dies?

Grief and love are two very similar emotions—if you are capable of love, you are capable of grief. Only a person who never loves never grieves. When you love someone, you feel a oneness and fulfillment with that person. (We talked about that in the first book of this series, *When Can I Start Dating?*) But you also open yourself up to the possibility for grief—when he or she breaks up with you, moves away, or dies. The relationship is over and that strong emotion of love mutates into equally strong grief.

Grief, then, results from the absence of opportunity to express love. Love expresses emotional oneness; grief expresses emotional separation. **Mourning** is the long, painful process of working through that grief. (In other words, *grief* is what we feel; *mourning* is how we respond to what we feel.)

Throughout *When Can I Start Dating?*, I keep reminding readers that the emotional roller coaster ride of adolescence is "normal." It's "natural" to feel up one day and down the next. It's okay to be ahead or behind other people your age in physical development. A million other teens are experiencing the same feelings.

But emotions do feel "abnormal" and "unnatural" when you're experiencing them for the first time. That's why the strong feelings of grief may seem frightening when you first feel the full force of this powerful emotion. Like other emotions, it's normal, natural, and okay. And like adolescent development, grief follows a general **pattern.**

Why don't you feel anything right after someone you love dies?

Stage One: Shock, Numbness, Disbelief (one to three days)[29]

"I just can't believe it!" is often our first reaction when we're told that someone we love has died. There's an immediate sense of shock and disbelief. Like "denial" in the dying process I described in chapter 4, disbelief **INSULATES** our emotions so we can deal with immediate demands: notifying friends and relatives, calling clergy, letting

the school know we'll be out for a few days, cleaning the house for visitors, and so on.

Once the initial numbness wears off, it's normal to cry—everything from watery eyes to uncontrollable sobbing. Crying is a healthy, emotional expression of grief, so don't feel that you're being "weak." And ignore ignorant clichés such as "Smile and the whole world smiles with you; cry and you cry alone."

It's not even unusual to feel anger toward the person for dying: "How dare you leave me to suffer like this!" You may feel angry at the medical staff for not saving your loved one's life—though the doctors and nurses did everything possible. And as I mentioned in chapter 4, it's not uncommon to feel angry at God—even if you're a devout believer. It's *okay*—as long as you are able to work through the anger.

Why do some people, when they've lost someone close to them, act like nothing happened?

It's not unusual, then, to feel these emotions, but it is unhealthy to **deny** them. For instance, Andrew's first child was born dead. When I visited him the next day, the burly factory worker proudly announced that he hadn't shed a tear. "My little girl's bouncing on Jesus' knee in heaven, so why should I be sad?"

But as months and years went by, Andrew's unresolved grief and anger began to come out as verbal and physical abuse against his wife (he tried to run her down with his truck), coworkers, and even his second child. Andrew had tried to plug up the mouth of a volcano of emotions. But the pressure simply blew a gaping hole out the side of the mountain.

Being a Christian doesn't exempt a person from grief and mourning. Jesus said, "Blessed are those who mourn, for they will be comforted" (Matthew 5:4). And **Jesus wept** at the tomb of His friend Lazarus even as He was planning to raise him from the dead (John 11:35). Jesus also went away by Himself to mourn the execution of John the Baptist, though He knew His cousin was in heaven (Matthew 14:13).

The apostle Paul doesn't glorify death either. He calls it an "enemy," but he assures his readers that if they believe in Christ as their Savior they will live forever (1 Corinthians 15:12–58).

The knowledge that we will see loved ones in heaven doesn't eliminate the intense pain of losing that earthly relationship! For instance, one January, I stayed home in Indiana to work on a book deadline while my family went to Walt Disney World in Florida. I knew they were in a "better place" and that I would see them soon, but I still missed them. The same is true of loved ones in a "better place." It doesn't decrease our longing to have them with us.

So, in review, it's normal to feel

- Shock
- Disbelief, denial
- Numbness
- Weeping, sobbing
- Anger

Allow these emotions to be expressed to those you can trust with your feelings—your best friend, family members, youth leader, or pastor.

Stage Two: Painful Longing and Preoccupation with Memories and Mental Images (one year or more)

We often think that the funeral is the hardest time for the survivors, so we may bring in food, visit the family, and attend the funeral. But after the service, we assume they've started to put their life back together.

After my grandfather died, I would walk into a room and almost believe he was there. Is that normal?

Actually, Stage Two becomes most intense between the second and fourth weeks after the death. The following experiences are **strong** for about the first three months, then gradually begin to **diminish** over the next six months to a year:

- Painful longing to be with and talk with the dead person
- Preoccupation with the death (you can't think of anything else)
- Memories of the dead person
- Mental images of the dead person
- The sense that the dead person is in the same room
- Sadness
- Tearfulness

- Inability to sleep
- Lack of concentration
- Loss of appetite
- Loss of interest in things you once enjoyed
- Irritability
- Restlessness

Again, these are normal reactions and nothing to be ashamed of. You also may have a difficult time maintaining the grades you're used to getting. Please don't view this as being a "failure" or "mentally undisciplined." Death puts a tremendous STRAIN not only on your emotions, but on your mind as well.

Fifteen-year-old Jason was driving a golf cart with his little brother, Justin, sitting in the back. Jason was driving faster than he should around the yard. He made a sharp turn, causing his brother to fly from the cart and smash his head into a concrete step. Justin died instantly. Jason, who apparently felt completely responsible, didn't speak to anyone for three weeks following the accident.

The sense of grief is even greater if the death was untimely (a teen or a young adult), through a tragic or violent means (accident, suicide, or murder), or to someone the survivor was very dependent on, such as a parent or best friend. In some cases, professional help may be necessary to move through the grieving process. (Resources and a listing of unhealthy grief symptoms are listed in Appendix B and on this series' website at www.jameswatkins.com.)

Author and counselor Norman Wright believes that the feelings of grief for a "normal" death can last up to two years, an accident up to three years, suicide four years, homicide five years, and the death of one's child for a lifetime. (When a parent dies, you lose your past, but when a child dies, you lose your future. Parents grieve each birthday of the dead child, at the date when he or she would have graduated from high school, gotten married, had children ... it never ends.)[40]

Funeral director Jim Stone suggests some ways to deal with that painful long-ing to **say good-bye** to the one you loved. "I always ask the living, 'Did you get everything said that you wanted to say?' If not, here are a couple sug-gestions: Write the deceased a letter telling her what you wanted to say but never said; seal it in an envelope and put it in the casket. Or, if appropriate, you may want to read it at the funeral.'

"I also suggest people leave a little memento—something that meant a lot between the two—in the casket. And if they don't want it to be seen by others, we'll put it out of sight, by the deceased's feet."

Grief seems to come in **waves.** One day you'll feel that you're finally over your loved one's death. But then you smell someone wearing his favorite cologne, you hear her favorite song on the radio, or a birthday or holiday comes along, triggering overwhelming grief again. These tidal waves of emo-tion are especially intense and painful at night when you're not distracted by school, after-school jobs, sports, watching TV, or hanging out with your friends.

When a death has affected the whole family, it's even harder because not every-one will be at the same place in the mourning process. You may feel angry at a family member if it seems he or she doesn't feel as badly as you do at the moment. Or you may feel a family member has grieved long enough and needs to be further along in the process. Remember that each family member will be dealing with the death personally, in his or her own way.

Be aware that the death of a child or a young person affects not only his or her family and friends, but the entire school, church, and community. To help stu-dents and parishioners deal with the death, many parents establish scholar-ships, plant trees in memory on public property, or sponsor athletic or artistic activities as memorials. In the case of high-profile deaths, such as school shoot-ings or famous people, the entire nation goes through a time of grief.

And the mourning process may not progress neatly from one stage to the other. John Irving in *A Prayer for Owen Meany* writes:

When someone you love dies, and you're not expecting it, you don't lose her all at once; you lose her in pieces over a long time—the way the mail stops coming, and her scent fades from the pillows and even from the clothes in her closet and drawers. Gradually, you accumulate the parts of her that are gone. Just when the day comes—where there's a particular missing part that overwhelms you with the feeling that she's gone, forever—there comes another day, and another specifically missing part.[41]

Author C. S. Lewis wrote about the death of his wife this way:

Tonight all the hells of young grief have opened again, the mad words, the bitter resentment, the fluttering in the stomach, the nightmare unreality, the wallowing in tears. For in grief, nothing "stays put." One keeps on emerging from a phase, but it always recurs. Round and round. Everything repeats. Am I going in circles, or dare I hope I am on a spiral?

But if a spiral, am I going up or down it?[42]

Accepting the fact that grief is a long—up to a five-year—process may be difficult. I said it in chapter 7 and it bears repeating: We live in an "instant" society, so we're tempted to think that our emotional state should **change** in 30 seconds or less. And that's just not so. Love doesn't grow in an instant—neither can it be instantly satisfied when a loved one dies. God could work an immediate miracle, but God often chooses to work in slow, deliberate, powerful ways.

Don't be afraid to turn to professionals for help during this difficult time. Your doctor may prescribe sleeping pills or tranquilizers so you can sleep. School counselors, youth workers, and pastors can provide emotional and spiritual support and suggestions for working through this time of loss. If they can't, they can refer you to those who can.

Do you ever stop hurting after someone you love dies?

Stage Three: Resolution and Resumption of Ordinary Life Activities (within one year of death)

Starting at about six months, most of us will begin getting back into our normal activities. We'll continue to be broadsided by occasional waves of grief as described in Stage Two. But these will become less and less frequent, though they may be just as **intense** when they recur.

Stage Three is summed up with

- Acceptance of the death
- Decreasing sadness
- The ability to recall past experiences with the deceased with pleasure rather than pain
- Resuming ordinary activities

A 15-year-old teen described his older sister's death as losing an arm. "Eventually the pain goes away, but you will always miss your arm. You can make adjustments and compensate for it, but you still have just one arm."

Do you always feel really bad about somebody's death?

If you haven't reached Stage Three after sufficient time, there may be **unresolved grief** • Some symptoms include: constant sadness, depression, anxiety, anger, and addictive or destructive behavior such as compulsive eating, drinking, working, gambling, or sexual activity. These are neither godly nor healthy. These behaviors numb our emotions and become a way of avoiding grief. (Remember Andrew who refused to grieve his stillborn child?)

If this is the case, many counselors suggest doing "grief work." Some suggest going back in your mind and reliving the death and all its emotions. Set aside time to grieve, to journal your thoughts about your loved one's death and what's happening inside of you. Consider joining a teen **support group** where you're free to share your feelings with those your age who have had a similar loss. "If you can't feel it, you can't heal it." Finally, don't be afraid to talk with a pastor, school counselor, or a professional therapist. God is the ultimate healer of hearts, emotions, and lives. His Word points us to His love for us in

Jesus, and He will lead us through our grief to feel again His love, joy, and power. Help is available!

In summary, grief is a normal—but sometimes confusing and uncontrollable— emotion. And mourning (dealing with grief) is a long, painful process. But remember: You *will* once again enjoy living and loving; you will get your appetite back; the pain will diminish; you will be able to sleep soundly again; and you will be able to enjoy pleasant memories of the deceased. And God will give you time and grace to move on.

A pizza commercial asks, "What do you want on your tombstone?" A deadly serious question when referring to the marble variety, but it's been answered in some lively ways!

In Ruidoso, New Mexico:

> *Here lies Johnny Yeast*
> *Pardon me for not rising.*

Can You Ever Really Be Prepared for Death?

In New Orleans, Louisiana:

> *This is what I expected,*
> *but not so soon.*

In Helena, Montana:

> *Anything for a change.*

Comedian W. C. Fields allegedly wrote his own epitaph:

> *All things considered, I'd rather be in Philadelphia.*

In Nantucket, Massachusetts:

> *Under the sod and under the trees,*
> *Lies the body of Jonathan Pease.*
> *He is not here, there's only the pod:*
> *Pease shelled out and went to God.*

Some tombstones chronicle the cause of death.

In Uniontown, Pennsylvania:

Here lies the body of Jonathan Blake;
Stepped on the gas instead of the brake.

In Albany, New York:

Harry Edsel Smith.
Born 1903—Died 1942.
Looked up the elevator shaft to see
if the car was on the way down.
It was.

On John Barrymore's monument:

See? I told you I was sick.

In Tombstone, Arizona:

Here lies Lester Moore.
Four slugs from a .44.
No Les. No more.

In Dodge City, Kansas:

Here lays Butch, we planted him raw.
He was quick on the trigger but slow on the draw.

In Leadville, Colorado:

Amos Rutledge hanged himself.
We would have done it for him.

Other marble markers are reminders to live life so we won't be remembered like these poor souls:

In East Dalhousie, Nova Scotia:

Here lies Ezekial Aikle,
Age 102,
The Good Die Young.

In Boston, Massachusetts:

Nearby these gray rocks,
enclosed in a box lies Mary Cox,
who died of smallpox
and none too soon for her husband, William Cox.

In Salt Lake City, Utah:

Rejoice!
She sleeps alone at last.

Somewhere in England:

Sir John Strange
Here lies an honest lawyer
And that is Strange.

So what do you want on your tombstone?

Two tombstones stand side by side in the **Pleasantville Cemetery** in Houghton, New York: one at attention guarding the remains of 24-year-old Samuel Glenn Root, a U.S. Marine Corps corporal; the other a silent witness to the violent death of Jean Root Aldrich, 31. Sam had three years to prepare for his death from AIDS. His sister, Jean, probably never felt the fatal blow to her neck.

Sam's medical file is a thick catalog of diseases: aspergillus pneumonia, cerebral toxoplasmosis, chronic sinusitis, cytomegalo viral retinitis, hepatitis, herpes simplex virus, oral thrush, and pneumocystis caninili (PCP). For the last year and a half of his life, Sam was completely blind because of AIDS-related diseases.

Jean didn't have the "luxury" of three years' notice. She had come out of her house to scold some neighborhood children for throwing rocks. Silently, a man who had been drinking all day crept up behind her, locked his fists together and struck her on the neck, rupturing a primary artery to her brain. The autopsy revealed that she died almost instantly from severe internal bleeding.

Yet out of these tragedies come lessons for all of us.

Value Life, Value Each Other

One of Sam's greatest concerns, after being diagnosed as HIV positive, was for good relationships between his parents, and among his four brothers and six sisters and his nieces and nephews. The normally soft-spoken young man became aggressive in making sure that **relationships** were right. "Hey, you guys, value life and each other."

He frequently asked his mother, "How are you and Dad getting along?" He tried hard to get to know his father, who, during Sam's childhood years, had been a long-distance truck driver during the weekdays and a pastor on the weekends.

Because none of us knows our date of death, we need to work at keeping our relationships with our parents, brothers and sisters, and friends in good shape. Will the last thing we remember saying to a deceased person be loving and kind, or hateful and hurtful? What will be the condition of our relationships at death?

We can remember the words of Scripture:

> Therefore each of you must put off
> falsehood and speak truthfully to

his neighbor, for we are all members of one body. "In your anger do
not sin": Do not let the sun go
down while you are still angry.
...Get rid of all bitterness, rage
and anger, brawling and slander,
along with every form of malice. Be
kind and compassionate to one
another, forgiving each other,
just as in Christ God forgave you.
(Ephesians 4:25-26, 31-32)

While in the HIV Unit of Balboa Navy Hospital, Sam was an eager guinea pig for experimental treatments. He felt that if he could **contribute** to AIDS research, somehow his life would have counted for something.

How will the world be different after I'm gone?

Here are 50 ways to let the world know that you lived.

1. Make people laugh.
2. Be a friend to people who don't have many friends.
3. Smile at everyone you meet.
4. Be generous with encouragement.
5. Build up people's self-esteem with sincere compliments.
6. Listen intently when people are talking; look them in the eyes.
7. Treat everyone you meet with love and respect (beginning with your mom and dad, brother and sister).
8. Forgive and forget.
9. Be polite and say "thank you" to waitresses and store clerks.

10. Read to those who can't read.

11. Better yet, teach people how to read.

12. Volunteer at a church.

13. Volunteer at a community organization.

14. Volunteer at a hospital.

15. Volunteer at a nursing home.

16. Volunteer at a school.

17. Teach a day care or Sunday school class.

18. Become a tutor.

19. Sponsor a child through an international relief organization.

20. Learn to save a life with CPR.

21. Give blood.

22. Sign a donor's card. (See the section of this chapter titled "Give Life at Your Death.")

23. Do things for others that they can't do, such as grocery shopping.

24. Or mowing their lawns.

25. Or walking their dogs.

26. Or housecleaning.

27. Or tuning up their cars, changing the oil, etc.

28. Or raking leaves.

29. Or putting in/taking out storm windows.

30. Or shoveling snow.

31. Be a pen pal to an overseas military or missionary child or teen.

32. Visit people in the hospital.

33. Visit people in nursing homes.

34. Write a poem or short story.

35. Write a letter to the editor.

36. Write to your legislators.

37. If you're 18 or older, register and vote.

38. Work for a political candidate.

39. Spread the Gospel.

40. Don't spread gossip.

41. Or STDs. (See the first book in this series, *When Can I Start Dating?*)

42. Share this book with a friend.

43. Better yet, help feed the Watkins family—buy copies of this book for all your friends.

44. Plant trees and flowers.

45. Become your family's official photographer and biographer.

46. Recycle.

47. Bake cookies for shut-ins.

48. Don't let friends drive drunk.

49. Help friends kick some habits (see chapter 3).

50. Send thank-you notes to people who have made your world a little bit different because they passed through it.

Joyce Landorf sums it up well: "The big question is not 'Will I die?' but, 'How shall I live until I die?'"[43]

Plan Ahead

There are many ways you can plan for your death. By doing some of the following, you can feel like you have *some* control over something you actually have little control over.

If you die and haven't made out a will, who will get all your belongings?

Sam began making plans for the rest of his life and beyond. He named Jean's children as his beneficiaries—the ones who would get the money from his life insurance at his death. Sam didn't have a **"last will and testament,"** but a will is especially important for parents. It allows Mom and Dad to select the family or person who will care for you in the event that they both die.

In my survey, one teen asked, "My mom's a single parent. If she dies, will I have to live in an orphanage?" That, again, depends on whether your parent has a will. When there is no will, the court system in most states determines where the children are placed and who gets any money and property.

If you have some valuable or sentimental things you would like to leave to certain family members or friends, it is best to have a will. But that's not always necessary for teens. If you write out your desires and have two witnesses sign the paper, that should hold up as directions for who gets your CD player, your tape collection, or guitar. Anything more complicated such as cash, property, children, etc., needs a professionally prepared will.

What's a living will?

Sam also made it known that in the event of cardiac arrest, he did not want to be resuscitated. This is often known as a **"LIVING WILL."** The following is a model drawn up by Concern for the Dying:

Death is as much a reality as birth, growth, maturity, and old age. It is the one certainty of life. If the time comes when I, [name], can no

longer take part in decisions for my own future, let this statement stand as an expression of my wishes, while I am still of sound mind. If the situation should arise in which there is no reasonable expectation of my recovery from physical or mental disability, I request that I be allowed to die and not be kept alive by artificial means or heroic measures. I do, however, ask that medication be mercifully administered to me to alleviate suffering even though this may shorten my remaining life. This statement is made after careful consideration and is in accordance with my strong convictions and beliefs. I want the wishes and directions here expressed carried out to the extent permitted by law. Insofar as they are not legally enforceable, I hope that those to whom this Will is addressed will regard themselves as morally bound by these provisions.[44]

Living wills are still controversial and not accepted in all areas. And many religious groups have strong opinions about these documents. Before signing one, you should carefully discuss the implications with your immediate family, your pastor, and your doctor.

Can I decide what happens to my body after I die?

Sam also made it known that he wanted his body to be cremated (burned to ashes) and for his funeral service to be a "home-going celebration."

Jim Stone, the funeral director we met in chapter 9, observes that "the trend is away from what we would call 'traditional' funeral services. Thirty years ago there was always one or two days of visitation and then a huge, long funeral. Today, especially on the two coasts, the trend is toward direct cremation with no calling hours and no funeral."

Time and money may be the reasons for the trend. A **TRADITIONAL FUNERAL** with embalming, casket, visitation hours, service, limos, burial vault, cemetery lot, and tombstone can cost several thousand dollars, while cremation is a fraction of the cost. To ship Sam's body from California, where he lived, to New York, where his family lived and where he wanted to be buried, would have cost thousands of dollars beyond that.

But Mike Stone believes that cremation may be more "costly" in the long run. "There's a real advantage to an open casket and a funeral service. Without being able to see and touch the dead body, your mind will play tricks on you. There's no confirmation that your loved one is really dead."

"That's why I object to the way cremation is handled in the Western world," Jim adds. "The body is simply shipped to the crematorium and, like Mike mentioned, there's no reality of the death. In India, however, the cremation takes place in a public place and the family often lights the funeral pyre. In South Africa, the funeral is often held at the crematorium. So in the Eastern world, the psychological need to see the body 'laid to rest' is satisfied."

Recall the account of Jesus' death in the Bible. It was important for the women who followed Him to honor Jesus' body by preparing it for burial and to say good-bye (John 19:38–20:1). Such a demonstration is a part of our natural grief process. But as Christians, we can rejoice that because of Christ's death and resurrection, fellow believers who have died are with Christ in paradise and we will be **reunited** with them.

Sam's parents initially objected to his cremation, then chose to follow their son's desire. You can make your wishes known about how you want your body disposed, such as in-ground or above-ground burial or cremation. But in most states, the final decision is in the hands of the immediate family. So if you have a strong preference, discuss it with your family.

Can I donate my body when I die?

Give Life at Your Death

Because Sam's body was infected with AIDS and the autopsy of Jean's body was used as evidence in the murder trial, donations of vital organs and tissue were impossible. But those are exceptional cases.

An estimated **20,000 Americans** need transplanted organs and tissue each year. Eighteen thousand are waiting for kidneys, 1,500 for livers, more than 2,000 for hearts. But less than one-tenth of those will receive organs donated at another's death.

The Uniform Anatomical Gift Act, which is recognized in all 50 states, allows a person to donate 1) all organs/tissues, 2) specific organs/tissues, or 3) the entire body for medical research. Donors of all ages are needed for bone, eyes, hearts, heart valves, kidneys, livers, lungs, pancreases, and skin. To become a donor at your death, you need to sign an organ donor card and have it witnessed by two people (your parents, if you're under 18, or your immediate family). The most important step is to discuss your wishes with your immediate family because they will have to be the ones to give consent for your organs and tissue to be donated.

All the costs of transplanting your organs and tissues will be paid by the receiver's health insurance—it won't cost your family anything for you to be a donor. And organ and tissue donation will not disfigure your body if your parents or immediate family want to have your body viewed at the funeral.

The following is an excerpt from a letter sent by the Indiana Organ Procurement

Organization, Inc. to the family of a young girl who died tragically. We'll call her Heather (not her real name).

We were able to use Heather's heart, kidneys, liver, and corneas for transplantation. I would like to give you some information on the recipients of your generosity.

Heather's heart was transplanted into a 59-year-old Indiana woman who had been extremely ill in the hospital prior to her surgery. She is doing well and looks forward to returning home to enjoy her retirement and her grandchildren.

Heather's liver was transplanted into a 50-year-old Indiana woman. Unfortunately, she did not survive the surgery. I'm sure that her husband and three grown children are grateful that she was at least given the chance for a better life. This is all she wanted.

Heather's right kidney was transplanted into a 32-year-old woman from Boston. She is doing very well, and is looking forward to the future with her fiance.

Heather's left kidney was transplanted into a 50-year-old man from California. He soon will be able to return to his career as a county administrator. He also enjoys traveling and movies.

Although I do not have any follow-up information on the corneas, they can be used to restore the sight of two people.

Hopefully this information will help lessen the pain that you have and can be a memory of Heather that you will cherish. Thank you again for offering us a very special opportunity to help many others to live longer with a much better quality of life. It is this thoughtfulness for others at a very difficult time which allows transplantation to occur.[45]

Does It Matter How We Live?

Both Sam and Jean had been raised in a Christian home (their father was a pastor), but as young people, they had turned their backs on God.

Sam was always sensitive, artistic, and a lover of music. Because he was more interested in reading than sports, teachers and classmates alike labeled him as "different." Sam joined the Marine Corps to prove his manhood, but eventually found the understanding and compassion he was looking for in the homosexual community.

After running away from home, Jean had survived as a prostitute while living with a drug dealer. She suffered the consequences of this dangerous lifestyle by being gang-raped, threatened at knife point, and brutally beaten. She had four children with four different partners.

It was a long road from a small country church parsonage in Wisconsin for both Sam and Jean.

After being diagnosed with HIV, Sam was called by God back to a LIVING FAITH. "I don't know why God wants me because I don't have much left to offer Him," Sam said. But he admitted that he was "loved back to the Lord" expressed through the unconditional love of his parents. "My mom told me 'You can hurt me—and you have—but you can never do anything that will keep me from loving you.'"

In the same way, his wayward sister was "loved back" by God. The Sunday before her murder, she had attended church with her family, seemed genuinely JOYFUL about her restored faith, and sang in a trio Sunday night with her mother and another woman. Monday, she brought her children to vacation Bible school and stayed to help. By 9:30 that night she was in the hospital morgue.

The forgiveness Jesus earned on the cross covers all our sins, and God is always seeking His lost sheep. But if we think we have all the time in the world to repent, we are wrong. No one knows the day of his or her death. We are reminded to live each day in readiness—not fear—for the moment of our death. As Christians, we TRUST Christ, who has defeated sin, death, and the devil for us.

The uncertainty of our life on earth is why the Bible says, "Now is the time of God's favor, now is the day of salvation" (2 Corinthians 6:2b). (We'll talk more about God and His promise of eternal life in chapter 18.)

How can you make the idea of death not so scary?

The idea of planning for your death may seem a little strange—it certainly did when I was a teen. It may even be frightening. One teen wrote, "Death is really scary because you never know when you will die."

But making some plans eliminates some of the questions asked: What will happen to my body after I'm dead? Will they take my eyes out even if I don't want it done? Who gets my CDs and stuff when I die?

Now that I'm married and have a daughter engaged to a police officer and a teenaged son with a driver's license, I guess I think more about death—especially before leaving on a trip. So in the top drawer of our fireproof safe is an "In Case of Death" file. It's **reassuring** to know that if Lois and I come face-to-face with a Mac truck: We have a will that will make sure our children are well cared for by a loving couple in our church; our organs will be donated (if they survive the crash); we'll have our favorite Scripture read and songs sung at our funeral; and what money we leave behind will go toward college scholarships at Indiana Wesleyan University.

I'm not planning to make national news this week ("Author and Wife Die in Fiery Car-Truck Crash"), but if I do, I'm as prepared as I can humanly be. These plans and the assurance that I remain **God's child** in life and death take the fear away.

But the most reassuring thoughts are found on Jean and Sam's tombstones. For a young woman suddenly murdered: "My Times Are in Your [God's] Hands." And for a young man who died in slow motion: "Death Has Been Swallowed Up in Victory."

So what do you want on your tombstone?

Jean's tombstone inscription creates as many questions as it answers: "My Times Are in Your Hands." The young woman we met in the previous chapter was murdered. But was it God's plan that she die in that manner at that time?

Why Do People Have to Die?

Why would an almighty God put us on earth just to die and put our family through that?

Why does God have to take away loved ones when you really need them here on earth at this time?

These questions are as old as Job. This godly man who is written about in the book of the Bible that bears his name lost his children, his health, and his considerable wealth. So for 36 chapters, Job and his three friends try to answer the haunting question, **"Why?"**

But the answer never comes. Instead, God thunders out even more questions: "Who is this that darkens My counsel with words without knowledge? Brace yourself like a man; I will question you, and you shall answer Me" (Job 38:2–3). "Would you discredit My justice? Would you condemn Me to justify yourself?" (Job 40:8).

After God spends four chapters (38–41) describing His power and control over creation, Job replies, "I know that You can do all things; no plan of Yours can be thwarted. You asked, 'Who is this that obscures My counsel without knowledge?' Surely I spoke of things I did not understand, things too wonderful for me to know" (Job 42:2–3).

The apostle Paul agrees with Job: "Oh, what a wonderful God we have! How great are His wisdom and knowledge and riches! How impossible it is for us to understand His decisions and His methods!" (Romans 11:33 TLB).

So at the risk of writing about things I don't understand and things far too wonderful for us to comprehend, let's look at what the Bible says about death.

God Holds Our Lives in His Hands

Throughout Scripture, we read that God has control over His creation—including the process of life and death. Job says of God, "I know that You can do all things; no plan of Yours can be thwarted" (Job 42:2). The psalmist declares, "Our God is in heaven; He does whatever pleases Him" (Psalm 115:3). The prophet Jeremiah writes, "Ah, Sovereign LORD, You have made the heavens and the earth by Your great power and outstretched arm. Nothing is too hard for You" (Jeremiah 32:17).

Death may be the result of sin, but God is able to **turn** this apparent **defeat into victory** through faith in Jesus Christ. The salvation of His chosen ones is a great miracle, a testimony of God's power and infinite love.

Why does death happen at the worst possible time?

God is aware of every aspect of our lives from the moment we are conceived to the moment we die:

> I praise You because I am fearfully and wonderfully made; Your works are wonderful, I know that full well. My frame was not hidden from You when I was made in the secret place. When I was woven together in the depths of the earth, Your eyes saw my unformed body. All the days ordained for me were written in Your book before one of them came to be. (Psalm 139:14-16)

The apostle Paul writes: "And we know that in all things God works for the good of those who love Him, who have been called according to His purpose" (Romans 8:28). This certainly doesn't imply that God keeps bad things from happening to those who love Him, but by His power He *does* bring good out of a bad situation.

Sometimes the facts seem confusing. God knows everything about each of us and has since before we were born—or even before the creation of the world. Why, then, would it make a difference what we do in life?

There is a difference between God's foreknowledge and His control of every act. God has given us considerable freedom to make decisions and choices—even when it means we make a wrong choice or sin. In fact, because of our sinful human nature, we don't have *free* choice because every decision is tainted by our sin. *We* can't choose the path of eternal life—God chooses us. But we do have the freedom to choose to say no to God's grace, which, sadly, some do.

God desires that all people believe and become part of His eternal family. He calls us to bow down to Him without forcing us to believe, and He accepts a person's choice to turn their back on Him. He helps us praise Him or we can curse Him. Most outrageous of all, **He loves all people**—both those who would love His Son and those who would nail Him to a cross and crucify Him! God is in control. He calls believers to faith as His Holy Spirit works through His Word. He also allows people to reject His grace.

If God knows the date of our death, what difference does it make how we live?

God created us to be thinking, rational beings. He wants us to make wise choices and be good caretakers of life. Our choices can either lengthen our lives or shorten them, as we discussed in chapter 3. Remember, alcohol abuse may take 10 to 12 years off a person's life! Is that God's will? Certainly not. Is it God's specific punishment for our actions? That's hard to say when we are well aware of the NATURAL CONSE-QUENCES of that behavior. Can God punish specific people for specific sins? Yes, but it is pretty difficult to apply God's specific action without His Word (the Bible) specifically explaining His judgment. Instead, we continue to rely on His grace and mercy amid all the difficulties of life, even when we don't have answers.

Why does God create disease that's meant to punish people, such as AIDS, but the disease kills innocent people too?

First, it is hard to say that God creates disease. He may allow new diseases to emerge if the natural laws are violated or as the world continues to decay under the influence of sin and Satan. Second, because we are all born sinful, no one is really "innocent." Most of our sins do not have a specific earthly punishment; some have consequences that seem like harsh judgments. Some people claim that AIDS is a punishment from God. While some "judgments" that occur may be the natural consequences of our behavior, they are not specific punishment from God! AIDS, for instance, is transmitted by blood-to-blood or blood-to-semen contact. So those who engage in practices that promote these conditions would be hardest hit—not because of divine justice but because of natural consequences. Thus, homosexual males and intravenous drug users who share needles were primary carriers of the disease in the United States, though the virus is spreading rapidly in segments of the heterosexual population as well.

Although on Judgment Day God will punish those who reject His offer of salvation (see chapter 18), the Bible is clear that He is "not willing that any should perish" (2 Peter 3:9 KJV). So tragic deaths are not a punishment from God. Jesus explains:

> Now there were some present at that time who told Jesus about the Galileans whose blood Pilate had mixed with their sacrifices. Jesus answered, "Do you think that these Galileans were worse sinners than all the other Galileans because they suffered this way? I tell you, no! ... Or those eighteen who died when the tower in Siloam fell on them—do you think they were more guilty than all the others living in Jerusalem? I tell you, no!" (Luke 13:1-3a, 4-5a)

If God is so powerful and personal, why isn't there heaven on earth? Why is there death? Why is there disease? Why is there evil?

Most of the tragedies of life are the ongoing result of the fall of creation recorded in Genesis 3. The PERFECT CREATION became marred by disease and death because sin entered the world. This world continues to spin in decay. Paul writes about the Last Day, when God will bring about the new heaven and the new earth:

> The creation waits in eager expectation for the sons of God to be revealed. For the creation was subjected to frustration, not by its own choice, but by the will of the

one who subjected it, in hope that
the creation itself will be liberated from its bondage to decay and
brought into the glorious freedom
of the children of God. We know
that the whole creation has been
groaning as in the pains of childbirth right up to the present time.
Not only so, but we ourselves, who
have the firstfruits of the Spirit,
groan inwardly as we wait eagerly
for our adoption as sons, the
redemption of our bodies.
(Romans 8:19-23)

Sometimes OTHER PEOPLE'S CHOICES cut lives short, such as Jean's murder and the school shooting in Littleton, Colorado, or an alcohol-related accident closer to home.

But where is God in these situations? I was recently reminded of this question by the testimony of a young woman who worked as a secretary in a large church across the street from the Federal Center in Oklahoma City. She was praising God that the church staff was in the basement having coffee and doughnuts when the infamous bomb exploded on April 19, 1995, killing 168 adults and children. While she and the staff were spared, why were equally devout adults and children not spared? Like Job, I don't have a clue. There is no earthly answer … and to pursue the answer only raises new questions.

By the power of the Holy Spirit in my life, I have come to believe—and trust—that God is active in His creation, including life and death. He has given people freedom to make choices that may prolong life or shorten it. Because we live in an imperfect world, disease and tragic events can end our lives.

So while God may know our date of death before our birth, it's hard to say that He in any way *causes* our death. Perhaps it will be cancer, a drunk driver, a murderer, defective brakes on our car, a tornado or earthquake, "old age," an airplane crash, "reaping" what we "sow," or one of a thousand different causes—but it won't be God. And it won't be His divine judgment. That comes at the end of time.

How could a loving God let my 5-year-old brother die?

The Bible doesn't give us the answers, but **God understands** our questions because He has suffered too.

- *Why do good people die so young?* I understand your question. I died at 33.
- *Why do some people die such painful deaths?* I understand your pain. I was beaten, whipped, and nailed to a cross.
- *Even though I know he's in heaven, I miss him so much here on earth.* I understand your grief. I left heaven to come to earth.
- *Why can't people just live forever and not have to die?* I understand the problem. I came to give you eternal life.

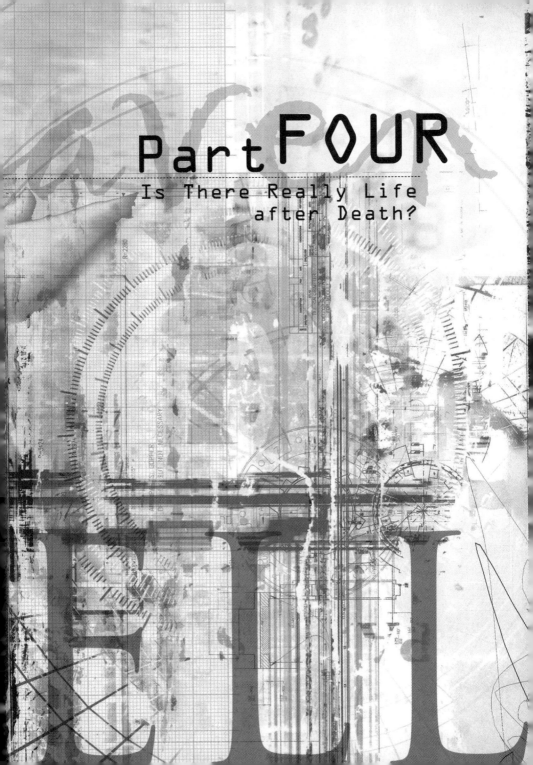

Part FOUR

Is There Really Life after Death?

I opened my eyes and looked around as I float-
ed face down in the cool, eerie silence of
Cadillac Lake. I couldn't feel any pain—or anything else—as I mentally checked myself out.
I'll just sit up and rest a bit, I thought.

Nothing happened.

Well, it's just like a football tackle when you

CHAPTER

13 Can Your Soul Leave Your Body before You're Dead?

have to wait to get your breath back. After a
moment, I put every ounce of strength and
mental energy into lifting my head out of the
water. Again, nothing!

I strained to turn my head so I could gasp for
air, but the surface of the lake always seemed
just a quarter-inch away from my mouth!

God, I need air! *Come on, don't panic. I'll just
wait for Mom and my brother to see me and
pull me out, and I'll be okay.*

Moments before, the sun had shown brightly
on the sparkling lake. I was home from college
for summer vacation and had been enjoying
the laughter and good times with my family at
our lakeside cottage in Michigan. I had
planned to swim underwater out to the raft to
give my mom, brother, and two sisters, who

were sunbathing, a good scare. I sprinted to the end of the dock and jumped off at a flat speed dive.

Instantly, my head smashed into something solid. I remember thinking, *This is just like the cartoons where Sylvester is chasing Tweety Bird on skis, and suddenly there's this telephone pole in the middle of the lake. POW! The skis keep going but the poor cat slithers down the pole into the water.* But this wasn't funny!

Come on, Mom! Notice me! I'm running out of air! I waited and waited. Gradually the sandy lake bottom began turning gray. My lungs felt as if they were being crushed by some invisible vise.

I tried to fight panic as I remembered my lifeguard training. If I passed out, I wouldn't be able to hold my breath any longer. My lungs would begin to fill with water and I'd be gone. My whole body felt as if it was going to explode with the pounding pressure in my chest.

Lord, I guess this is it, I prayed. *I guess I'm going home. But what makes me deserve heaven? What have I ever done? I've never really shared my faith with the guys in the dorm or the people at work. God, I've failed You.*

But then I sensed God saying, "Don't worry, you're My child." My body began to relax as I felt this beautiful peace and joy. An unbelievable, powerful love seemed to push the pain out of my chest and fill my whole body. Everything had now turned black and yet there was a feeling that Christ was right beside me. And then, a blinding light as I struggled to open my eyes.

Mike Carlton's story is incredible! According to the paramedics who revived my friend, he had been in the water long enough for severe brain damage or death. Doctors can't explain why Mike walked out of the hospital two weeks later in perfect health when he should be paralyzed or dead. Mike believes God brought him through this close call with death. Or did Mike actually cross the line between life and death and return from the dead?

IS THERE REALLY LIFE AFTER DEATH?

Can people be brought back from the dead?

Mike is not alone in his experience. Thousands of people come within a breath of death each year, and one-fifth of those resuscitated report some kind of sneak preview of the afterlife!

Medical science defines death as 1) the absence of clinically detectable vital signs; 2) the absence of brain-wave activity; and 3) the irreversible loss of vital functions. Because of this, we are really talking about NEAR-DEATH EXPERIENCES (NDEs) when we discuss stories like Mike's. Many NDEs have several things in common:

- The sensation of leaving one's body
- Passing through a dark tunnel
- Seeing a bright light
- A sense of love and peace
- Seeing one's life in review
- Meeting friends and relatives who have died
- Making a painful decision to return to earthly life or experiencing disappointment at being revived

Not everyone has all of these experiences, however, and NDEs aren't limited to these common experiences. Some have reported "floating in a blue bubble," "being held by a giant hand," "straddling a beam of light and touring the uni-

PAGE
156

verse," and seeing "cities of gold."

And not all of the NDEs are pleasant experiences. Some report "being horrified by nude, zombie-like people," and others report "a lake of fire" and the "smell of burning sulfur." An Intensive Care Unit nurse I interviewed reports an unusual case. A 32-year-old woman began bleeding uncontrollably, lost all blood pressure, and went into a coma during a difficult childbirth. While she was being resuscitated, she later reported that she saw her doctor playing cards with a red creature with horns. "They were gambling for my soul," she suggested later. The doctor won.

Some researchers believe there are many more negative experiences than are reported for many reasons: the experience is so frightening that the patients block it out of their memory; they're ashamed to admit they saw hell rather than heaven; or they fear people will think they're crazy.

But NDEs are nothing new! Ancient Egyptians *created* these near-death experiences as an initiation rite for priests of Osiris and would-be pharaohs by sealing candidates in mummy coffins for eight minutes. (Archaeologists speculate that many slaves died while cult members tried to determine the exact time that one could survive without oxygen and still be revived.) *The Egyptian Book of the Dead* documents these experiments and describes journeys down dark tunnels opening up to bright lights. *The Tibetan Book of the Dead* and *The Aztec Song of the Dead* describe similar phenomena.

The apostle Paul reports what some might consider an NDE in 2 Corinthians 12:2–4:

```
I know a man in Christ who four-
teen years ago was caught up to the
third heaven. Whether it was in
the body or out of the body I do
not know—God knows. And I know
that this man—whether in the body
or apart from the body I do not
```

know, but God knows—was caught up to paradise. He heard inexpressible things, things that man is not permitted to tell.

Is there proof that people have out-of-body experiences?

Raymond Moody, a medical doctor, was one of the first to attempt to study NDEs scientifically. His two best-selling books, *Life after Life* and *Reflections on Life after Life*, were based on interviews with 150 patients who had close calls with death.

But scientifically verifying NDEs is impossible. First, the studies are based on an extremely limited number of cases. Second, because of patient confidentiality, there is no way to know if the patient is a reliable witness. Is he or she a truthful, mentally stable person? (I'm convinced that Mike Carlton is such a person.) Or has he or she also seen Elvis recently? Third, the only proof is the patient's subjective memory of a personal experience. There are no other witnesses to verify that this experience did indeed occur. And we all know how stories can become exaggerated after many tellings.

Possible Explanations

Russel Noyes of the University of Iowa believes that the sensation of leaving one's body is caused by *transient depersonalizations*. In other words, people experiencing near-death events become emotionally detached from their bodies. This allows them to handle a situation without panic and to initiate life-saving measures. Sigmund Freud, the famous psychiatrist, first held this theory claiming that "our own death is indeed unimaginable and whenever we make an attempt to imagine it, we can perceive that we really survive as spectators."[46]

A similar phenomena is *autoscopic hallucination* in which people see a MIRROR IMAGE of themselves because of the pain associated with brain tumors, strokes, or migraine headaches. One out of 50 people have experienced this, including President Abraham Lincoln during a bout with migraines.

But transient depersonalization and autoscopic hallucination can't explain away every out-of-body experience. The first scientific report appeared in an 1889 issue of the *St. Louis Medical and Surgical Journal,* where a medical doctor fell into a coma, lost all signs of life, and was pronounced dead by another doctor, S. H. Raynes. After reviving, the doctor reported that while apparently dead, his "non-physical body resembled that of a jellyfish ... and that his body passed through those of others in the room without contact."[47]

The sensation of passing through a dark tunnel can be caused by OXYGEN LOSS (hypoxia). Dr. Marshall Goldberg has documented near-drownings (like Mike Carlton's) where patients saw darkness, then a bright light. But Dr. Melvin Morse, author of *Closer to the Light,* claims that many of his patients had adequate oxygen while experiencing NDEs.

One's "life in review" can be explained by **brain activity**. Under stress or grief, the hypothalamus gland in the brain will signal the pituitary gland to secrete the hormone ACTH, which has been found to cause one's life to flash before one's eyes, either from infancy to present or in reverse from most recent to early life.

The most dramatic proof that NDEs can be caused by brain activity was documented by Wilder Penfield, known as the father of neurosurgery. In the 1930s, Penfield discovered that poking the right temporal lobe of the brain (just above the right ear) produced out-of-body experiences. Since the brain has no feeling, Penfield conducted these experiments with patients who were wide awake! Patients spoke of leaving their bodies or being "half in and half out." They also reported "seeing God," hearing beautiful music, seeing dead friends and relatives, and "seeing their life flash before them."

Dr. Karlis Osis thought perhaps these NDEs were the "product of a sick or defective brain," but his research reveals that "the clearer the patient's mind, the more strong this experience was."[48] When he tried to explain the experiences with drugs or high fevers, he made some other interesting discoveries. Of those having NDEs, only one in five were taking drugs and only one in 10 had medical conditions (such as brain tumors) that might possibly cause hallucinations; fewer than one in 10 had high fevers.

While many near-death experiences can be explained away physically or medically, there are some cases that seem to have no such explanation. Michael Sabom, a cardiologist, discovered that 32 of his patients claim to have actually left their bodies and watched their own resuscitation. While these patients were not medically trained, each person accurately and with great detail could describe the **intricate** procedures performed on him or her while he or she was apparently unconscious.

People who have near-death experiences also seem to know other things they shouldn't humanly know. In 1926, Sir William Barrett's book *Deathbed Visions* reported people who were critically ill and who had not been told of a loved one's recent death. Yet when the patients "returned from death," they described meeting that loved one "on the other side." Many similar stories of talking with dead friends and relatives have been told in more recent books and articles.

But do these "unsolved mysteries" prove there is life after death? I don't think so. Here's why:

1. If NDEs are a sneak preview of the afterlife, they should present a fairly similar picture. While there are many people who do see dark tunnels and bright lights and feel intense love, there are many others who see things as diverse as blue bubbles, zombies, giant hands, and lakes of fire.

2. If NDEs are a sneak preview of the afterlife, they should reveal the same divine presence. However, NDEs seem to be based on one's religious and cultural background. Protestants see Christ. Catholics see Christ, Mary, or other saints. Hindus see Lord Krishna. Atheists and agnostics, however, only see bright lights or feel great love.

Many NDEs also contradict the Bible's teaching of the afterlife. For instance, Satan is not the "red creature with horns" the bleeding woman reported, but "a fallen angel" according to Scripture. Betty Eadie's best-selling tale of her NDE, Embraced by the Light, contains a dangerous mixture of New Age philosophy and Scripture. (We'll talk more about that in Are There Really Ghosts?, the third book in this series.)

For the person who has lived through a **brush with death**, the experience is real, whether it can be explained away by modern science or not. But the claim that it proves anything about the afterlife just doesn't seem valid. There are still too many questions and inconsistencies in the experiences—and too many contradictions with the message of the Bible—for us to identify what these experiences are. To quote St. Paul, "I do not know, but God knows."

Of the top 10 questions asked in my survey of teens, six related to the number one question: "Is there really life after death?"

The number two question was, "Do you really come back as someone or something else?" "Where do you go when you die?" ranked sixth, followed by "Are

14 Once You're Dead, You're Dead, Right

you able to come back as a ghost and haunt people?" "What is heaven like?" and "What is hell like?"

Other questions included:

- "Do you get a second chance at life after you die?"
- "Do you go back to where you were happiest?"
- "Is everything after death hunky-dory?"
- "What kind of research is being done on this?"
- "Can you believe in a lot of stuff dealing with death, such as reincarnation, ghosts, life after death, etc.? And if you do believe in these things, aren't you just afraid to deal with death?"

In the next three chapters, we'll look at some possible answers to those questions. (We'll save ghosts and communication with the dead for the third book in this series, *Are There Really Ghosts?*, which deals with the supernatural.)

The first theory about life after death is

The Big Nothing

Two students asked, "I don't believe in God, so I don't believe in heaven or hell, but I'm wondering, where do I go?" and "Is there a heaven or hell, or are you just blackened out for eternity?"

The position that atheists and humanists take is summed up in the statement, "Once you're dead, you're dead." Those who believe that our lives are nothing more than highly EVOLVED PROTOPLASM reject the idea of an eternal soul.

Do you just rot in the ground?

According to the Big Nothing theory, we do simply "rot in the ground" with absolutely no awareness or consciousness. After death there is simply nothing, nonexistence, non-being, zip, zero, nada. We're no different than a dead flower or a flattened raccoon along the road.

Atheists, humanists, and evolutionists, however, have a difficult time explaining how the "mere mass of cells" that is the human body can create, dream, plan, design, communicate facts and ideas, and experience emotions such as love and hate, joy and sorrow.

The majority of people do believe that there is something—a soul, a spirit, an image of God, an "essence"—that lives within this 100-or-so-pound blob of protoplasm we call our bodies. And the majority of people believe that whatever it is will live for **eternity.** "Where" we live is the subject of the next few chapters.

Rob Holt* was very … well, very, very different. As a high school student, he claimed to be an extraterrestrial. He always wore cotton in his ears to filter out the "earth frequencies," which he claimed were higher pitched than those of his **native planet.** Rob refused to participate in swimming during phys. ed. because his "high-voltage energy field" would

CHAPTER

15 Do You Really Com Back as Someone o Something Else?

turn us mere humans into boiled lobsters if he got into the pool with us.

But the biggest difference was Rob's god, **"Kosgro McOrlo Excelsior."** He, she, or it lived in a gold gift box in his locker. And for just 25 cents, classmates could take a peek at this god in a box.

I've lost touch with this unique student whom most of us thought had lost touch with reality. Was Rob really crazy? There are three possibilities:

> 1. Rob was no alien—and he knew it. The whole "Kosgro McOrlo Excelsior" routine was a scam to rip off students' lunch

*Not his real name.

PAGE
164

money. Instead of a court-appointed psychiatrist, Rob deserved an Oscar for "Best Portrayal of an Alien by a High School Student"—or at least a warning from the Better Business Bureau.

2. Rob was no alien—but he really thought he was. In this case, in-patient treatment at the state mental hospital would be in order.

3. Rob really was an alien. The rest of us were merely ignorant earthlings who were unaware of Rob's remarkable powers.

Simply because something is hard to believe doesn't make it false. We've all experienced events that cause us to exclaim, "You're not gonna believe what happened!" Say, for instance, you sink a basketball from half court. How can others know it's true? There are several questions that relate to the incredible basket—and Rob.

1. Is Rob a credible person? Can we believe what he says? Can people believe you when you say you sank a basketball from half court?

2. Are Rob's stories consistent with one another? Are they consistent with other stories of extraterrestrials? In the case of the basketball shot, do you tell the same story, with the same details, each time?

3. Can other people verify Rob's story? Are there reliable eyewitnesses to his supernatural powers? Were your friends or the coach watching when you sank the basket?

4. Do Rob's "history" and "observations" of the universe agree with historical or scientific evidence? Your basket can't be "scientifically" proven because that would demand that you could readily repeat the feat each and every time under the same conditions (you probably can't). But you could have "historical" proof (eyewitnesses, videotape, or an article in the school paper) that it did happen at one point in time. Others can go to the school and see the basketball hoop and ball.

If there are major flaws in Rob's story, then it's doubtful that Rob is really a space-traveling follower of Kosgro McOrlo Excelsior. But if his story stands up to reasonable investigation, then we need to give it serious consideration. The same kind of questions need to be asked about REINCARNATION.

A good number of people do believe in reincarnation—two-thirds of the world's population and, according to a 1981 Gallup poll, 38 million Americans.

Reincarnation teaches that our souls are a part of the essence of God and we come back to earth in different forms until we reach the highest level of "god-ness" or "universal consciousness" or "nirvana." Hindu tradition teaches that we get a brand-new body with each cycle. Buddhists, however, believe that each new body is made up of the same kind of "skandhas," which, loosely translated, means "goo." The majority of modern reincarnationists—and virtually all ancient peoples who followed this belief system—hold that humans can be recycled as rocks, frogs, trees, or sacred cows.

Do you really come back as someone else?

Americanized reincarnation, however, teaches that humans come back only as humans. (We'll talk more about this later.)

An important "doctrine" of reincarnation is "karma"—a cosmic "Chutes and Ladders" game. This "force" determines if we come back as a member of the royal family or as a rootworm. If we live a good life and learn our lessons well, we will come back at a higher "caste" or level of society. If we're dirty, rotten scoundrels, we slide down a few notches.

Are Reincarnationists Credible People? Can We Believe What They Say?

American reincarnationists include doctors; lawyers; college professors from such universities as Cambridge, Harvard, and Yale; politicians; and theologians. So we're not talking about people with shaved heads and peach sheets selling flowers in airports. Reincarnation in America has become increasingly popular because of the best-selling books by **Edgar Cayce**, "the father of American reincarnation," and by actress/dancer *Shirley MacLaine* (*Out on a Limb* and *Dancing in the Light*).

Are these credible people? Cayce, allegedly, learned his high school lessons by sleeping on his books and dropped out after seventh grade. Apparently, he sould have slept on his history books a bit longer. (We'll read more about his "Cayce history" later.) MacLaine claims that under "psychic acupuncture" she is able to talk to animals, trees, and her "higher self." If someone at your school started talking about these things, she'd find herself taking to the school psychologist.

MacLaine, if she is credible, should also be accurate—since she is in touch with "infinite wisdom." She argues that Jesus taught reincarnation by preaching, "As you sow, so shall you reap." First, the passage refers to reaping what we sow in *this* life—not in some future life. And second, Jesus never said it! It was the apostle Paul (Galatians 6:7).

MacLaine also states that the theory of reincarnation is recorded in biblical manuscripts but the religious Council of Nicea in A.D. 553 deleted all mention of reincarnation from the Bible. Again, she's in error. The Council of Nicea met in A.D. 325 and dealt with Origen's idea that souls were formed before conception. At issue was the creation of the soul, not reincarnation—and removal of portions of Scripture was never discussed at the council. Such serious errors undermine MacLaine's credibility.

Author and speaker John Van Auken is the director of the Edgar Cayce organization. His website claims he is an expert in Egypian, Hebrew, and Christian mysticism. In his book, *Born Again...and Again*, he stretches his credibility **thread-thin** when he speaks of mythological animals, such as centaurs (half horse/half man), satyrs (half goat/half man), sphinxes (half lion/half man), and mermaids and mermen as real beings that roamed the early earth.

Are these people credible witnesses? You decide. But according to MacLaine, credibility is irrelevant! Read on.

Can Reincarnationists Prove Their Stories? Are There Reliable Eyewitnesses to Reincarnation?

Like the out-of-body experiences we discussed in chapter 13, reincarnation experiences are impossible to verify because there are absolutely no outside witnesses to verify an individual's story. Modern reincarnationists try to avoid any JUDGMENT or analysis of their claims because as MacLaine writes: "... reality [is] only what one person perceive[s] it to be. Everyone's perception of reality [is] valid."[49]

In other words, because Rob believes Kosgro McOrlo Excelsior exists, it therefore exists. And he, she, or it is just as real as this computer I'm typing on—at least according to MacLaine. Then again, she wouldn't admit that this P.C. is real because she believes "reality [is] only what one believe[s] it to be anyway. That would make all perceived realities real."[50]

Everything is "basically part of what we called 'God.'"[51] So according to MacLaine, the questions of "proof" and "reliability" are irrelevant because there is no such thing as truth and falsehood, good or evil. People have their own truth, so it's not possible to judge another's truth.

On the contrary, Jesus Christ's resurrection (not to be confused with reincarnation) **has reliable, verifiable, historical evidence and witnesses.** (We'll talk more about this in book three of this series, *Are There Really Ghosts?*) So while faith is important, I question any belief that depends completely on the unverifiable testimony of its followers.

IS THERE REALLY LIFE AFTER DEATH?

DO YOU REALLY COME BACK AS SOMEONE OR SOMETHING ELSE?

Are Reincarnationists' Stories Consistent with One Another?

As I pointed out about near-death experiences, if they are real, there should be some consistency in the stories. The same test must apply to reincarnation. Hindu reincarnation is different from the Buddhist version, and the American version contradicts both of the Eastern versions.

Do you really come back as something else? ... as a fly? ... as a buffalo?

When reincarnation came to America, the idea of humans possibly becoming **flies or sacred cows** just didn't sell. So the system of belief was simply modified to appeal to an America audience: "No, you don't come back as a lower life-form. In fact, you just keep coming back as better and better people." Ralph Waldo Emerson, the famous author and "transcendental meditation" guru, promoted this idea as "up and onward forevermore."[52]

Edgar Cayce, however, disagreed with Emerson. He saw his past lives as a "constant roller coaster, up and down; now a high priest and virtual ruler of Egypt, then a humble warrior in Troy or a ne'er-do-well scout in colonial America."[53]

Do you get to pick what you come back as?

Western reincarnationists not only reject the Hindu "doctrine" of going backward in the next life, they also reject the basic purpose of reincarnation—KARMA. As we noted, MacLaine believes we "choose" our next life rather than having karma seal our fate.

Do people remember who they were in their past life?

There is also great disagreement when it comes to whether the reincarnated can know their past lives. Some, like Geddes MacGregor, argue that one cannot know about his past lives. "Deprivation of memory [is] essential to new development and growth."[54] Other adherents claim that "inherited memory" or "collective unconsciousness" is remembering the life of some ancestor that has been genetically transmitted rather than an individual remembering his own past. Still others, like Edgar Cayce and Shirley MacLaine, write very specific accounts of their own lives. (We'll talk about Cayce's "lives" later.)

The Westernized version of reincarnation rejects two-thirds of the ancient Eastern philosophy by rejecting any downward movement and the concept of karma. And that's fine because they believe there is no truth or falsehood—just personal revelation.

Do Reincarnationists' "History" and "Observations" Agree with Historical or Scientific Evidence?

Shirley MacLaine and other reincarnationists try to make the Bible prove reincarnation when Hebrews 9:27–28a is quite clear: "Just as man is destined to die *once,* and after that to face judgment, so Christ was sacrificed once to take away the sins of many people." Instead of this clear biblical teaching, MacLaine and company write of Jesus and His disciples being born again—and again and again. They take several verses in the Gospel of John completely out of context:

In reply Jesus declared, "I tell you the truth, no one can see the kingdom of God unless he is born again."

"How can a man be born when he is old?" Nicodemus asked. "Surely he cannot enter a second time into his mother's womb to be born!"

Jesus answered, "I tell you the truth, no one can enter the kingdom of God unless he is born of water and the Spirit. Flesh gives birth to flesh, but the Spirit gives birth to spirit. You should not be surprised at My saying, 'You must be born again.'" (John 3:5-7)

Jesus speaks specifically against reincarnation when He makes the **distinction** between physical birth and the new spiritual life that is ours as the Holy Spirit works through the water and God's Word in Baptism. Men can reproduce only human life, but the rebirth Christ speaks of is from the Holy

Spirit. (We'll talk more about this in chapter 18.)

Another section that reincarnationists like to misinterpret is John 8:57–58 where Jesus is proclaiming His eternal nature as God. He begins by claiming to have known Abraham, who lived centuries before.

> "You are not yet fifty years old," the Jews said to Him, "and You have seen Abraham!"
>
> "I tell you the truth," Jesus answered, "before Abraham was born, I am!"

At issue is Jesus' timelessness as God. Because Christ was fully God and God has existed for eternity, then it follows that He was alive before Abraham. Proving that Christ is eternal doesn't prove in any way that we are. In addition, Jesus doesn't say "I *was*," but "I *am*"—which means He **continuously exists** as the same person of the Trinity.

Reincarnationists point also to Christ's transfiguration (Matthew 17:1–5; Mark 9:2–8; Luke 9:28–36), where He meets with Moses and Elijah, as proof of reincarnation. Again, it merely points out that Moses' and Elijah's spirits were very much alive in God's presence (we'll talk about that concept in chapter 16), but it doesn't prove anything about reincarnation. Those who try to make the Bible prove reincarnation also point to references of John the Baptist being the reincarnation of the Old Testament prophet Elijah.

> The disciples asked Him, "Why then do the teachers of the law say that Elijah must come first?"
>
> Jesus replied, "To be sure, Elijah comes and will restore all things. But I tell you, Elijah has already come, and they did not recognize him, but have done to him every-

> thing they wished. In the same way
> the Son of Man is going to suffer
> at their hands."
> Then the disciples understood that
> he was talking to them about John
> the Baptist. (Matthew 17:10-13)

Was John the Baptist, the messenger of Christ, *actually* Elijah? The archangel Gabriel, who announced his birth, prophesied, "He will be a man of rugged spirit and power *like* Elijah, the prophet of old" (Luke 1:17 TLB, italics mine). John the Baptist himself denied he was Elijah in John 1:21. When Jesus states, "John appeared, and if you are willing to understand what I mean, he *is* Elijah" (Matthew 11:13–14 TLB, italics mine), He is reminding His listeners that John is the one PROPHESIED to fill Elijah's Old Testament role of calling people to repentance. John was, therefore, a fulfillment of the prophecy in Malachi 4:5–6.

The apostle Paul was aware that "the time will come when men will not put up with sound doctrine. Instead, to suit their own desires, they will gather around them a great number of teachers to say what their itching ears want to hear. They will turn their ears away from the truth and turn aside to myths" (2 Timothy 4:3–4).

Are MacLaine and her followers credible when they distort the Bible and take it out of context?

Edgar Cayce, in whom Shirley MacLaine and her medium, Kevin Ryerson, place so much faith, was far from a FAITHFUL HISTORIAN. The "sleeping prophet," as he was known, fell into trances in which he would "recall" past lives. His followers would record his observations. He claimed his first life was in Atlantis, the mythical "lost continent." But it was far from mythical to Cayce. Atlanteans were "not yet in the flesh, were thought-forms, disembodied energy."[55] These sexless thoughts eventually became male and female people who traveled the seas on high-tech hovercrafts at more than 700 miles per hour. When the dinosaurs became a nuisance, the Atlanteans simply disintegrated them with cosmic ray guns. Where is Atlantis today? According to Cayce, the five islands went to war with nuclear weapons, causing massive earthquakes and tidal waves that buried the land at the bottom of the Atlantic Ocean.

Cayce said he went on to live as the high priest Ra-Ta in Egypt, a medicine man in Persia, and the infamous Xeon of Troy, who opened the gates of the city to the Trojan Horse. He then appeared in Judea as Lucius the Cyrene, one of the prophets and teachers noted in the New Testament (Acts 13:1). And he claimed he came back to "indulge his sexual appetites" in France and the colony of Virginia as the father of illegitimate children.

Although Cayce's stories are hard to believe, remember that is not sufficient evidence to write them off. But these "**Cayce histories**" have no historical evidence. Plato wrote of the "lost continent of Atlantis," yet there is no solid historical or archeological evidence for such an advanced civilization. Other Cayce histories are absolutely incorrect. For instance, Cayce claimed that Jesus Christ had previously been Adam and then Enoch. That would be impossible because Adam and Enoch were alive at the same time! Cayce also claimed to have been Lucius, ministering in Judea, when scriptural records place Lucius far north in Antioch of Syria.

Can someone with so little accuracy be trusted? No.

Will we have the same scars and problems we had in another life?

Ivan Stevenson, a psychiatrist who served at several universities and hospitals, believes he has "proof" that reincarnation explains everything from birthmarks to cravings during pregnancy. Stevenson believes birthmarks are actually scars from previous lives. He claims to have examined more than 200 cases where gun shot wounds, knife cuts—even beheadings—in other lives have shown up as birthmarks. He also believes that PHOBIAS (irrational fears of heights, water, insects, etc.) are actually memories of past lives when one was killed by falling off a cliff, drowning in a shipwreck, or being bitten by a black widow spider. "Love at first sight," he says, occurs when two people who were lovers in a past life meet in this life. According to the psychiatrist, child prodigies who excel at piano were probably concert pianists in another life.

Heredity is a much more believable explanation for birthmarks—which are not "scars" at all, but clusters of melanin (the pigment that produces skin color). And most fears can be traced easily from earlier experiences rather than delving into past lives. And we offer a more rational theory for love at first sight in the first book in this series.

John McTaggart of Cambridge University believes reincarnation can't be explained away by heredity. He teaches that eternal souls search for fetuses that are most like their previous bodies. He describes it as a man looking for the **right size hat** to wear. So it is not heredity that creates a certain characteristic or talent; instead, according to McTaggart, an eternal soul just happened to find a body that suited his or her talents and abilities.

Reincarnationists also try to explain away heredity with an "electric architect" or "astral body." Harold S. Burr writes of his experiments at Yale in *The Electric Patterns of Life*. Dr. Burr claims these eternal blueprints are the "electrodynamic field" of the "real body" of a person upon which the physical body is built. Hindus speak of "chakras" and Buddhists of "lotus centers" that connect the astral bodies to the physical bodies. Acupuncture (sticking long needles into these points) supposedly brings healing by reconnecting these two bodies. So Burr believes that chromosomes and DNA that control fetal development are actually controlled by this over-riding electrodynamic field.

None of these explanations satisfies our innate knowledge that there is a creative God who made each of us unique and gave each body a living soul.

More Questions

Reincarnation has been seriously **questioned** for thousands of years. The early church leader Tertullian argued against reincarnation because it couldn't account for the population explosion of his time. Now, several billion people later, the question is still unanswered. Ivan Stevenson suggests that souls are simply being recycled at a faster rate in our century or that more sub-human animals are being reincarnated as humans. (So *that's* where all the endangered species are going!)

Others ask why we aren't more advanced if souls continue to grow closer to this "universal wisdom." Why do crime rates continue to skyrocket? Why have there been more wars in this century than in any other? Reincarnationists like

MacLaine would simply argue that "there are only *perceptions*." The Hiroshima and Nagasaki atomic blasts and the Columbine High School shootings were only perceptions?

Reincarnation is based on a non-scriptural, imprecise, eerie system devised by humans. In contrast, God's Word speaks of the `true`, `sure`, and `eternal` `hope` of the resurrection of all believers in the same way Jesus was raised. Jesus was resurrected as Himself, not another person or thing. His resurrection is historically verifiable.

So is reincarnation a credible belief system? After a careful examination of the evidence, I've come to the conclusion that it doesn't make sense.

In the hit movie, *My Girl,* Vada, the undertaker's 10-year-old daughter, tells her best friend, Thomas J., her idea of heaven:

I think that everyone gets their own horse or their own bike or car or whatever it is they like to ride. And all they do is ride them and eat whatever they want all day long. And every-

16 Is There Really a Heaven?

body is best friends with everybody else, and when they play sports, there are no teams so no one gets picked last. And you don't have to be scared of that. Actually, nobody's scared of anything. And nobody has allergies or gets sick. And they take care of each other, like friends. And ... nobody has to die.[56]

Is there really a heaven with golden streets—for Vada and Thomas J. to ride bicycles?

The "Soul" Survivor

Before we discuss where we go when we die, we first have to discuss what part of us survives after death.

In the story of creation, we read, "And the LORD God

formed the man from the dust of the ground and breathed into his nostrils the breath of life, and man became a living being" (Genesis 2:7). The Bible teaches that God created us not only with a physical body, but an **eternal soul**. Throughout Scripture, the inspired authors wrote of humans as having souls or spirits. (See 1 Thessalonians 5:23.)

Jesus taught the existence of the soul when He commanded His followers to "love the Lord your God with all your heart and with all your soul and with all your strength and with all your mind" (Luke 10:27). He made it clear that the body and soul are separate when He spoke of persecution: "Do not be afraid of those who kill the body but cannot kill the soul" (Matthew 10:28a).

The Bible's definition of **death**, then, is separation of the soul from the body. We see death explained this way throughout the Old Testament (see Job 14:10). We see the same concept in the New Testament when Jesus raises Jairus' daughter from the dead: "He took her by the hand and said, 'My child, get up!' Her spirit returned, and at once she stood up" (Luke 8:54–55). While Jesus was on the cross, He "called out with a loud voice, 'Father, into Your hands I commit My spirit.' When He had said this, He breathed His last" (Luke 23:46).

The Bible, then, clearly states that each of us has an eternal soul or spirit that becomes separated from our earthly body at death.

Why does God make us go through life on earth if He knows that heaven is much better?

Does this mean that, as one author claims, "death is a friend to be embraced"? From the creation of life in the book of Genesis to the destruction of death in the book of Revelation, the importance of physical, earthly life is stressed. In the gospels we find Jesus and His disciples healing the sick and even raising the dead. If our earthly life were merely something to be endured before we could enjoy heavenly life, then it would be absolutely cruel for Christ to heal the sick—and even more so to bring the dead back to life. Christ's earthly ministry **validates** the importance of physical life.

Death, on the other hand, is viewed throughout Scripture as "an enemy" (1 Corinthians 15:26). It is the result of sin, which perverted God's perfect creation. Paul writes that we live in a body of death (Romans 7:24) and face death all day long (Romans 8:36). But God doesn't leave us to die. He wants all people to be saved and to live. Our earthly life is good because God is part of it and provides us the opportunities to share His love in Christ with others. The apostle Paul wrote about the positives of life and death:

> For to me, to live is Christ and to die is gain. If I am to go on living in the body, this will mean fruitful labor for me. Yet what shall I choose? I do not know! I am torn between the two: I desire to depart and be with Christ, which is better by far; but it is more necessary for you that I remain in the body. (Philippians 1:21-24)

If "to live is Christ," then life is **not meaningless.** For instance, I have a friend who suffered severe heart failure. As a result of blood not getting to her brain, she's somewhat brain damaged. To make things even more tragic, she had a brilliant mind before her cardiac arrest. With the dazed expression of someone who is mentally impaired, she keeps asking, "Why didn't God just take me? Why did He leave me here like this?" I have no answer except to tell her, "God puts real value on life and living—regardless of our 'quality of life.'"

If God didn't care about our earthly life, He wouldn't give us the many good gifts of food, clothing, jobs, medicine, and so much more that affects our physical well being.

Amazing Grace

In addition to the concept of the soul or spirit, we need to understand how souls are **judged** in the afterlife. Did Mother Teresa go to heaven because she gave unselfishly to help the poor? Did Adolph Hitler go to hell because he was responsible for the deaths of more than 10 million people? The Bible's answer is no.

> For it is by grace you have been saved, through faith—and this not from yourselves, it is the gift of God—not by works, so that no one can boast. (Ephesians 2:8-9)

> You see, at just the right time, when we were still powerless, Christ died for the ungodly. Very rarely will anyone die for a righteous man, though for a good man someone might possibly dare to die. But God demonstrates His own love for us in this: While we were still sinners, Christ died for us. Since we have been justified by His blood, how much more shall we be saved from God's wrath through Him! (Romans 5:6-9)

> Whoever believes [in Jesus Christ] and is baptized will be saved, but whoever does not believe will be condemned. (Mark 16:16)

Therefore, Mother Teresa and Adolf Hitler go to heaven or hell based on belief in Jesus Christ—not on their actions.

How spiritual do you have to be to get to heaven?

Our eternal fate is not determined by our good or bad actions or our degree of "spirituality." (We'll talk more about this in chapter 18.) Look at Ephesians 2:8 again: "For it is by grace you have been saved, through faith—and this is not from yourselves, it is the gift of God." **Faith** is God's gift to us. Because we have faith and believe in Jesus as our Savior, we have forgiveness of sins and eternal life. When we talk about the "believing dead" and the "unbelieving dead," it is not the "good" dead and the "bad" dead, but those who believe in Christ and those who reject Him.

At what age can you go to heaven or hell?

God's grace extends even to those who are young (babies, children) or not mentally competent (the mentally retarded or mentally ill) when there is saving faith—even the simple faith of a child. Our God is loving and gracious. He puts no age limit on heaven; He requires no "comprehension quiz" to "get in."

Sheol/Hades/Heaven

On my survey, young people wanted to know: Where do souls go after death? … to a holding tank? … to wait in the grave? … to a waiting room? Isn't there a place between heaven and hell?

Unfortunately, there is no chapter in the Bible entitled "Everything You Ever Wanted to Know about the Afterlife." We are left to piece together clues that are scattered throughout Scripture. We do know that when we die, our bodies return to **dust**, but the souls of those who believe go to be with Christ in heaven (Ecclesiastes 12:7; John 17:24).

In Luke, Jesus tells a story about the rich man and Lazarus (Luke 15:19–31). It describes those who have died as being separated by a great gulf, with the believing dead on one side "being comforted" and the unbelieving dead on the other side in "torment" and "anguish." We call the place of comfort *heaven* or *paradise* (Luke 23:43) and the place of anguish *hell* (Matthew 10:28; 25:41). There is no biblical evidence to support a place of waiting (sometimes called *purgatory*) or any other alternative to heaven or hell.

Why will believers go to heaven? When Jesus died on the cross, the curtain in the Jewish temple—which separated the people from God—ripped from top to bottom (Matthew 27:51). This announced that Jesus' sacrifice paid for our sins and removed the barrier between us and God. No longer would people have to bring sacrifices for the forgiveness of their sins. Christ was the PERFECT SACRIFICE and through Him, all believers have forgiveness and eternal life (Hebrews 10).

Can you see what's happening on earth from heaven?

It is difficult to say what state we are in after death. St. Paul refers to "those who have fallen asleep" (1 Thessalonians 4:15), and Jesus refers to the daughter of Jairus as "sleeping" (Mark 5:39). Yet we are still alive in Christ. In Hebrews, the writer speaks of a great cloud of "witnesses" (Hebrews 12:1). Because "witnesses" most often refers to martyrs who gave a firm testimony of faith—and even died because of that testimony—we interpret this word to mean "models" who give us courage and hope. Neither the rich man nor Lazarus seems to have had any option to "observe" life on earth (Luke 16:19–31). Rather the rich man seems to be recalling situations from his earthly life. Nor did Lazarus (Mary and Martha's brother) or even Jesus indicate an awareness of earthly life. If we watch earthly events while we are in heaven, it may cause sorrow, which we are told will no longer exist.

Resurrection Power

The story of the afterlife doesn't end with the believers in heaven with Christ and the unbelievers in hell. The Bible also says that all the dead bodies—which, after centuries, are nothing but dust—will be "resurrected" or brought back to life. Daniel prophecies, "And many of those whose bodies lie dead and buried will rise up, some to everlasting life and some to shame and everlasting contempt" (12:2 TLB). Jesus taught, "Do not be amazed at this, for a time is coming when all who are in their graves will hear His voice and come out—those who have done good will rise to live, and those who have done evil will rise to be condemned" (John 5:28–29).

The apostle Paul writes:

> The body that is sown is perishable, it is raised imperishable; it is sown in dishonor, it is raised in glory; it is sown in weakness, it is raised in power; it is sown a natural body, it is raised a spiritual body. (1 Corinthians 15:42-44)

What will our heavenly bodies be like?

God teaches that "flesh and blood cannot inherit the kingdom of God" (1 Corinthians 15:50). The natural body we live in while on earth will perish (1 Corinthians 15:44, 42), and in heaven we will receive a distinct heavenly body (1 Corinthians 15: 40). This heavenly body will be like **Christ's resurrected body.** Christ's resurrected body wasn't a ghostly form—it could be touched and could eat a meal (Luke 4:38–43). In fact, passages in Isaiah and Revelation suggest that we'll do a lot of eating in heaven. (Now that *will* be heaven—a seven-year feast and we won't gain a pound!)

Is there sex in heaven?

One part of heavenly bodies that didn't appeal to me, as a teen, was the unisex design: "Jesus replied, 'Marriage is for people here on earth, but when those who are counted worthy of being raised from the dead get to heaven, they do not marry'" (Luke 20:34–35 TLB).

What?! No sex?! But Paul says that an earthly marriage is a human "echo" of the union of Christ and His bride, the Church (see Ephesians 5:31–32). So earthly marriage is just a small sampling of the pleasures of heaven. (I deal with this in more detail in *When Can I Start Dating?*, the first book in this series.)

Are there real mansions in heaven?

There could be. We might have wonderful surroundings … but they may not be anything like what we consider "nice" on earth. It may be far better. Or these new bodies may be the "mansions" Jesus promises: "In My Father's house are many rooms; if it were not so, I would have told you. I am going there to prepare a place for you. And if I go and prepare a place for you, I will come back and take you to be with Me that you also may be where I am" (John 14:2–3).

Paul speaks of these "homes" as new bodies:

> For we know when this tent we live in now is taken down—when we die and leave these bodies—we will have wonderful new bodies in heaven, homes that will be ours forevermore, made for us by God Himself, and not by human hands. How weary we grow of our present bodies. That is why we look forward eagerly to the day when we shall have heavenly bodies which we shall put on like new clothes. For we shall not be merely spirits without bodies. (2 Corinthians 5:1-3 TLB)

How can I enjoy heaven if my friends are in hell?

Several teens asked, "How can I enjoy heaven if I know that some of my friends and family are in hell?" Job, who had a lot of questions, may have the answer: "Death consumes sinners as drought and heat consume snow. Even the sinner's own mother shall forget him. … No one will remember him any more" (Job 24:19–20 TLB). The joy of being in **God's presence** will remove any concerns for the matters of earthly life.

What is heaven like?
Is heaven really a literal place with gold streets and all?

Like the mansions, we don't know exactly what heaven will be like. Most scriptural references are **figurative**, like those in the book of Revelation.

Then I saw a new heaven and a new earth, for the first heaven and the first earth had passed away, and there was no longer any sea. I saw the Holy City, the new Jerusalem, coming down out of heaven from God. ... And he carried me away in the Spirit to a mountain great and high, and showed me the Holy City, Jerusalem, coming down out of heaven from God. It shone with the glory of God, and its brilliance was like that of a very precious jewel, like a jasper, clear as crystal. It had a great, high wall with twelve gates, and with twelve angels at the gates. On the gates were written the names of the twelve tribes of Israel. There were three gates on the east, three on the north, three on the south and three on the west. The wall of the city had twelve foundations, and on them were the names of the twelve apostles of the Lamb.

The angel who talked with me had a measuring rod of gold to measure the city, its gates and its walls. The city was laid out like a square, as long as it was wide. He measured the city with the rod and found it to be 12,000 stadia in length, and as wide and high as it is long. He measured its wall and it was 144 cubits thick, by man's measurement, which the angel was using.[57] The wall was made of jasper, and the city of pure gold, as pure as glass. The foundations of the city walls were decorated with every kind of precious stone. The first foundation was jasper, the second sapphire, the third chalcedony, the fourth emerald, the fifth sardonyx, the sixth carnelian, the seventh chrysolite, the eighth beryl, the ninth topaz, the tenth chrysoprase, the eleventh jacinth, and the twelfth amethyst. The twelve gates were twelve pearls, each gate made of a single pearl. The great street of the city was of pure gold, like transparent glass.

I did not see a temple in the city, because the Lord God Almighty and the Lamb are its temple. The city does not need the sun or the moon to shine on it, for the glory of God gives it light, and the Lamb is its lamp. The nations will walk by its light, and the kings of the earth will bring their splendor into it. On no day will its gates ever be shut, for there will be no night there. The glory and honor of the nations will be brought into it. Nothing impure will ever enter it, nor will anyone who does what is shameful or deceitful, but only those whose names are written in the Lamb's book of life.

Then the angel showed me the river of the water of life, as clear as crystal, flowing from the throne of God and of the Lamb down the middle of the great street of the city. On each side of the river stood the tree of life, bearing twelve crops of fruit, yielding its fruit every month. And the leaves of the tree are for the healing of the nations. No longer will there be any curse. The throne of God and of the Lamb will be in the city, and His servants will serve Him. They will see His face, and His name will be on their foreheads. There will be no more night. They will not need the light of a lamp or the light of the sun, for the Lord God will give them light. And they will reign for ever and ever. (Revelation 21:1-2, 10-22:5)

This text gives some hints, but no clear picture of what it will be like, for "now we see but a poor reflection as in a mirror; then we shall see face to face" (1 Corinthians 13:12).

Are there animals and pets in heaven?

We really don't know for sure. Another figurative account in Isaiah says:

The wolf will live with the lamb, the leopard will lie down with the goat, the calf and the lion and the yearling together; and a little child will lead them. The cow will feed with the bear, their young will lie down together, and the lion will eat straw like the ox. The infant will play near the hole of the cobra, and the young child put his hand into the viper's nest. They will neither harm nor destroy on all My holy mountain, for the earth will be full of the knowledge of the LORD as the waters cover the sea. (Isaiah 11:6-9)

An even stronger suggestion comes from Romans 8:22, where Paul writes "the whole creation has been groaning" and waits "in hope that the creation itself will be liberated from its bondage to decay" (v. 21). It may be that the **new heaven and new earth** will have resurrected believers and animals as well. Since animals were present in the first perfect world, it isn't unreasonable to expect them to be present in the recreated new earth.

Are there literally gates of pearl and golden streets in heaven?

Again, let me say with absolute certainty—I have no idea! It's possible that the prophets used symbolism and similes because they couldn't put the INCREDIBLE BEAUTY of heaven into human words. The best they could do was write of a place so fantastic that they use giant pearls for city gates and pave streets with gold. It is a place where we will be in the very presence of God. The most beautiful part will be the opportunity to see our glorious Savior and marvel at His incredible beauty and worship and praise Him forever.

If it is literal, it will be incredible. If it's not literal, it will be way beyond incredible!

A Texas newspaper reports:

Rev. Bill Lane who ... preaches "hellfire, damnation, and brimstone" added something new to his "preachin." Suddenly the lukewarm evangelist became one of the

17 Is There Really a Hell?

hottest evangelists in the country. Literally! He set himself on fire while giving a sermon on hell. The idea caught on like wildfire and soon [he] was known to millions as the Flaming Evangelist.

Already, Rev. Lane has set himself on fire 75 times and has only been burned badly once. [He] wears a specially treated undershirt and shirt to prevent the fire from burning through.

While the flames are raging, Bill points to the crowd

with a flaming finger and shouts, "You may
not like what you are seeing, but imagine
this for eternity."[58]

Is there really a hell?

Let's examine some ideas.

The Roman Catholic Church teaches that PURGATORY is an intermediate
state between heaven and hell.

> In purgatory, souls suffer for a
> while in satisfaction for their
> sins before they can enter heaven.
> The principal suffering of these
> souls consists in the pain of expe-
> riencing, on one hand, an intense
> longing for God and, on the other,
> a realization that they are hin-
> dered from possessing Him by rea-
> son of their past sins. Unlike the
> souls in hell, they are certain of
> one day seeing God. They can be
> helped, moreover, by the prayers of
> the faithful on earth, and espe-
> cially by offering of Mass.[59]

But Protestants would protest (thus the name) this doctrine on several points.
First, the word *purgatory* is not found in the Protestant or Catholic Bible.
Second, the Protestant Reformation was founded on the concept of salvation
by grace—not human works. Even the Catholic Bible teaches: "For by grace
you have been saved through faith; and that not of yourselves, for it is a gift of
God; not as the outcome of works, lest anyone may boast" (Ephesians 2:8–9
The Catholic Bible).

And there is no need for additional purification, as the Catholic Bible states: "If we acknowledge our sins, [Christ] is faithful and just to forgive us our sins and cleanse us from *all* iniquity" (1 John 1:9, The Catholic Bible, italics mine).

Protestants have other problems with the arguments for purgatory. The doctrine was not taught by the Catholic church until the seventh century, so early church fathers did not subscribe to such a teaching. And it would seem that the thief crucified with Jesus would need to spend some time in purgatory for his many sins, yet Jesus PROMISES the repentant criminal, "Today you will be with Me in paradise. This is a solemn promise" (Luke 23:43 TLB).

While there is nothing specifically about purgatory in Scripture, there are some very detailed descriptions of hell.

Hell

As we discussed in chapter 16, the bodies of the unbelieving dead are left in torment and anguish until the final Judgment Day.

Are you really judged?

> Then I saw a great white throne and Him who was seated on it. Earth and sky fled from His presence, and there was no place for them. And I saw the dead, great and small, standing before the throne, and books were opened. Another book was opened, which is the book of life. The dead were judged according to what they had done as recorded in the books. The sea gave up the dead that were in it, and death and Hades gave up the dead that were in them, and each person was judged

according to what he had done. Then death and Hades were thrown into the lake of fire. The lake of fire is the second death. If anyone's name was not found written in the book of life, he was thrown into the lake of fire. (Revelation 20:11-15)

Is there really fire in hell?

Is this a real, literal "lake of fire"? Again, let me say with absolute certainty—I have no idea!

Jesus spoke of *hell* throughout the gospels. The Greek word He uses is *Gehenna*, which comes from the Hebrew word *Ghi-Hinnom* or *Valley of Hinnom*. Located just west and southwest of Jerusalem was a literal Gehenna. Here, parents had forced their children to walk through fire fueled by brimstone in worship to the false god Molech (2 Kings 23:10; Isaiah 30:33). During Christ's time, **Gehenna** was a constantly burning landfill. Often garbage would lodge in the rocks above it and breed maggots. This may explain the description of "the fire of gehenna," "where 'their worm does not die, and the fire is not quenched.' Everyone will be salted with fire" (Mark 9:48–49).

Throughout Scripture, *fire* is used as a symbol for something greater or more fearful. So if *hellfire and brimstone* are symbols, then hell is something far worse than literal burning. So I wouldn't take any comfort in thinking hell is not literal. If it's not literal, it's something unspeakably worse!

We know one element of hell is complete separation from God. Even here on earth when things seem bad, Christians rejoice that Christ is always with us (Matthew 28:20; Hebrews 13:5). But for the unbelievers who will find themselves in hell, no one or nothing will be available to **buffer** them from the pain and sorrow.

> This will happen when the Lord Jesus is revealed from heaven in blazing fire with His powerful angels. He will punish those who do not know God and do not obey the gospel of our Lord Jesus. They will be punished with everlasting destruction and shut out from the presence of the Lord and from the majesty of His power.
> (2 Thessalonians 1:7-9)

Seven times the Gospels speak of hell as "outer darkness ... the place of weeping and gnashing of teeth": Matthew 8:12; 13:42; 13:50; 22:13; 24:51; 25:30; and Luke 13:28.

Jesus warns us that the "cursed ones"—those who have refused His gift of salvation—"will go away to eternal punishment; but the righteous to everlasting life" (Matthew 25:46). In other words, the punishment of unbelievers will be the exact same length as the reward of the believers—eternity (Daniel 12:2; Matthew 18:8; Mark 3:29; 9:44–48; Jude 13).

Do you get a choice between heaven and hell?

The good news, however, is that God "is not willing that any should perish" (2 Peter 3:9 TLB). "For God so loved the world that He gave His one and only Son, that whoever believes in Him shall not perish but have eternal life. For God did not send His Son into the world to condemn the world, but to save the world through Him" (John 3:16–17).

Max Lucado writes, "God does not send people to hell. He simply honors their choice."[60] C. S. Lewis put it this way: "There are only two kinds of people in the end: those who say to God, 'Thy will be done' and those to whom God says 'Thy will be done.'"[61] (We'll talk about this in the next chapter.)

In response to the part of my survey concerning "a question I have about the possibility of life after death," a 15-year-old girl wrote:

I don't have a question, but I have a question for you. I believe that the afterlife is not just a possibility, but that there is life in either heaven or hell. Jesus Christ is my Savior and Lord and I know where I am going. Do you?

18 I Don't Have a Question

It's a question we all need to answer. I wish I could meet this bold believer and assure her, yes, I believe in Jesus Christ as my Savior and Lord and I know where I am going.

Believing in Jesus Christ as Savior is more than just "fire insurance." (Who wants to burn in hell?) It's more than "getting into" heaven and living forever. It's a love relationship between God and you. Here's a simple explanation of how God brings us into this relationship.

1. Love comes from God.

    ```
    Dear friends, let us
    love    one    another,
    for love comes from
    God. (1 John 4:7a)
    ```

Many people think that God is only interested in rules. But God is all about love. Jesus, God the Son, reminds us of the most important "rule":

" 'Love the Lord your God with all your heart and with all your soul and with all your mind.' This is the first and greatest commandment. And the second is like it: 'Love your neighbor as yourself.' " (Matthew 22:37-39)

"Okay," we say. "That sounds good." But on our own we are powerless to love like that.

Those who say, "I love God," and hate their brothers or sisters, are liars; for those who do not love a brother or sister whom they have seen, cannot love God whom they have not seen. The commandment we have from Him is this: those who love God must love their brothers and sisters also." (1 John 4:20-21 NRSV)

2. The power to love comes from God.

Everyone who loves has been born of God and knows God. Whoever does not love does not know God, because God is love. This is how God showed His love among us: He sent His one and only Son into the world that we might live through Him. This is love: not that we loved God, but that He loved us and sent His Son as an atoning sacrifice for our sins. (1 John 4:7b-10)

Anything we have done that is not loving separates us from a loving God. We don't have to murder or commit armed robbery to "sin." Sin is simply breaking God's commandment to fully love Him and others.

> **If we claim to be without sin, we deceive ourselves and the truth is not in us. (1 John 1:8)**

But God's only Son, Jesus Christ, died and rose again to atone for our unloving behavior (see 1 John 2:1–2). *Atone* means to make *at one*. When we confess our lack of love (sin) and believe that Christ has died and risen for our sin, we are forgiven and are "at one" with God and His love (see 1 John 1:9).

If anyone acknowledges that Jesus is the Son of God, God lives in him and he in God. (1 John 4:15)

3. The power to love unselfishly comes from God.

Love from God is not earned—it is a free gift—but it is *learned.*

> **No one has ever seen God; but if we love one another, God lives in us and His love is made complete in us. (1 John 4:12)**

We get to know God and His love better through reading His love letter (the Bible), talking to Him (prayer), and being with those who also love Him (the church). And the better we know God, the easier it is for us to obey His commandment to love Him and others.

> **This is love for God: to obey His commands. And His commands are not burdensome, for everyone born of God has overcome the world [of sin]. (1 John 5:3–4a)**

If you'd like more information about strengthening your faith relationship with God, talk to your minister or Christian youth leader. Or you can write me in care of the publisher (the address is in the introduction to **The Why Files** on page 12) or e-mail me at whyfiles@jameswatkins.com.

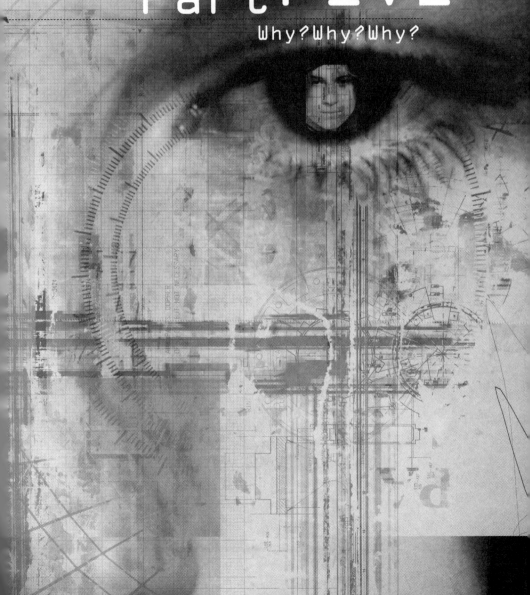

Part FIVE

Why?Why?Why?

The little "SEND" icon on my e-mail program scares me! Once I click it, there's no way to take back what I've written to a friend or to the newspaper office where my weekly column is published. The message speeds to the newsroom where the editor makes sure it's not libelous and sends it to composition.

19 I Still Have a Question

Within a few hours, it is printed and being read by thousands of readers (or is house-breaking new puppies). There's no chance to say, *Wait a minute! I really didn't mean that! What I meant was ...*

I have that same fear with the three books in this series. What I've written is being edited, typeset, printed, bound, and shipped off to local and online bookstores as an authoritative answer to questions about adolescence, death, and the supernatural.

I've tried to verify and document each answer through personal interviews and hundreds of hours of researching printed and online material. One professor at Ball State University kept telling us graduate journalism students: "Verify, verify, verify! If your mother says she loves you, verify it!" I think I've done that. (I finally had to explain to the city librarian that I wasn't a sex addict or psychic serial killer, but I was writing three books. I'm not sure she was convinced as I toted armloads of sex, death, and occult books out the door every two weeks.)

Still, I feel like I've only scratched the surface of these deep, deep subjects. That's why you'll find books listed in the Endnotes that will give you more in-depth information. Plus, this series' website will give you up-to-date resources. Check it out at www.jameswatkins.com. And feel free to e-mail me at why-files@jameswatkins.com if you have a comment or a question.

So while I've tried to honestly answer the hundreds of different questions on a thousand surveys, I still have many of my own questions about love, death, and God. (I'm certainly not like the 15-year-old who wrote on the survey, "I have no questions. I know everything.")

With that in mind, none of these thoughts are "final copy." God is always stretching His children spiritually and mentally so their attitudes, values, priorities, perspectives, knowledge, and relationships are constantly revised and updated to conform more to Jesus, "the author and perfecter of our faith" (Hebrews 12:2). And He also promises to be with us for the stretch.

Let's just consider these three books as a "rough draft." Okay? Thanks.

Dear Friend,

I pray that you may enjoy good health and that all may go well with you, even as your soul is getting along well.

(3 John 2)

Jim

A Special Message to Parents

"Why is Mom so humongous sad?" 3-year-old Paul kept asking as we drove to my wife's girlhood home in Wisconsin.

"Because her dad, your grandpa, died," I tried to explain, but soon realized it wasn't getting through any more effectively than "We're not there yet. It's a long trip to Wisconsin."

His 8-year-old sister, Faith, tried to help with, "He's gone to heaven!"

Psychologist Maria Nagy has discovered from her research that children under the age of 5 don't believe death is final. That's why Paul asked, "When is he coming back from heaven?"

Between ages 5 and 9, youngsters begin to accept the finality of death but don't understand that they themselves must eventually die. Older children and teens gradually begin to realize that they themselves are mortal.

How can we help our children and young people deal with the reality of death?

Preparing

In the cases of cancer or AIDS, parents have time to prepare children for the death of a loved one. But in the event of an auto accident or stroke, death comes suddenly, with no warning. That is why our children need to be prepared for death.

The responsibility rests on us parents. Some schools offer "death education" classes, but most of our young people's learning about death comes from their peers. (Remember that horrible playground dirge: "Never laugh when the hearse goes by. You may be the next to die. The worms crawl in, the worms crawl out ...")

The evening news provides many opportunities to bring up the subject with our children: local auto accidents, murders, and suicides; deaths of famous people; international war casualties—the list is endless.

I hope this book will be read by both young people and parents and encourages them to work together through the many questions that surround this often taboo subject.

Telling

Announcing the death of a loved one to your child or teen may be one of the hardest jobs of parenting. Often we ourselves are feeling intense emotion. It's difficult to tell our children that one of their grandparents—and one of our parents—has died. Medical and mental health professionals agree that we should "ease into" the announcement. Here's a typical "script."

Often it begins with nonverbal communication: your sad expression or tears.

"I'm afraid I have some very sad news." **You're beginning to prepare your children for the bad news. You're also giving them freedom to feel sad concerning the news.**

"Remember how the doctors were really worried about Grandpa's high blood pressure?" **You've planted the thought that something very serious has happened to their grandparent. Notice how each phrase brings worse news.**

"Grandpa had a very bad stroke, and the doctors did everything they could. [Pause] But Grandpa died."

Easing into such an announcement is not the same as dishonesty. Not being straightforward, even with small children, can be dangerous.

In chapter 9, we discussed the importance of using the "D-word" (death). If we tell a small child that a grandfather has "gone to sleep," the child may become afraid to go to bed or will expect Grandpa to wake up soon. If we say, "God took him," the child may become angry at God for being so cruel (see chapter 12). Never teach a child something he or she will have to un-learn later in life.

Listening

Elizabeth Richter, author of *Losing Someone You Love,* interviewed teens who had lost a brother or sister to death. "The most obvious need expressed by all the young people I spoke with was a desperate desire to be heard and for their feelings to be accepted, not judged, not ignored. Their questions did not always require answers, but they longed for compassion and understanding."[62]

One of the greatest temptations for me, as a parent, is to try to "fix" the situation. It is important to resist an urge like this. As I mentioned in chapter 9, teens—and adults—need our ears more than our mouths. Allow them to express themselves without our "answers" and clichés. When they ask a direct question, a direct answer is appropriate, but also allow them to ask questions you cannot answer.

Grieving

In the past, people were told not to cry out loud at funerals. Mourners were urged to dry their eyes, be brave, be strong, and not express grief. Tranquilizers were used to keep emotions under control. Today medical and psychological studies have revealed the importance of "good grief."

Children and teens look to adults for clues about how to grieve. That's why it's important that we are open with our own feelings and questions. Encourage your child or teen to cry when he feels like crying, to be silent when he doesn't want to talk. Allow her to work through, in her own way and time, the stages of mourning described in chapter 10.

Amy Hillyard Jensen, whose 9-year-old drowned and whose 23-year-old was killed in an auto accident, suggests we should "deliberately take time to grieve. Review mementos. Play nostalgic music. Look at pictures and read old letters. One therapist often recommends one hour a day—a grieving prescription."[63]

During the mourning process, we need to make sure our young people eat well and get regular exercise. Often, those in mourning lose their appetites and become inactive. A good diet and exercise actually speed up the recovery process through biochemical changes that reduce depression.

Be watchful of destructive or "pathological grief" described in the next appendix. If these symptoms persist, get your children to professional help: a pastor, school counselor, youth worker, physician, or mental health professional.

Being There

As I mentioned in chapter 9, often just "being there"—without answers and clichés—is valuable support.

It's always important to spend time with our children and young people, but it's absolutely essential to spend special time with them following a death. Take your child out to eat—just dad and son, or mom and daughter. Work on projects together. Do whatever you can to bring the two of you together for an hour or two of uninterrupted time. (I talk more about this in the appendix of book one in this series, *When Can I Start Dating?*)

If your teen has lost a friend or classmate, funeral director Jim Stone urges parents to go to the funeral home with him. "Your young person needs your support during this very difficult time," Stone says.

Keep in mind that the mourning process can take up to five or more years to work through. Most of all, assure your young person that grief is a very normal emotion and is shared by every other person who has lost a loved one.

Finally, know that faith is the most important part of dealing with death. Life and death are both of God—for God sent Jesus to bring resurrection and eternity to all who believe in Jesus as Savior.

A Special Message to Teachers and Youth Leaders

More and more attention each year focuses on teen deaths from alcohol-related accidents, school shootings, suicide, and AIDS. As teachers and youth leaders, we will be called on more and more to provide answers and support to our young people as they confront the realities of death and dying.

As I mentioned in chapter 10, *grief* is the emotion of loss; *mourning* is the lengthy process of dealing with grief. Grief is a normal, natural response to losing someone we love. I believe our task, then, is to help our students or teen groups understand the normal, natural stages of grief.

Marge Kavanaugh is a counselor at Central Noble High School in northern Indiana. In February, three students were killed in an automobile accident. In May, one of the school's favorite teachers died of a heart attack—while at school. "The deaths hurt all of us—staff and students. But some positive things came out of it," she noted as we talked about the deaths.

Marge and her staff were prepared for such a tragedy with a crisis plan that had been formulated by the school district two years before the school's first death.

The simplified plan includes these steps:

1. Building principal is designated to form a crisis management team in each school to deal with crisis.

2. Superintendent or designee will be in charge of media and outside

operations (ministers, counseling agencies).

3. Inform staff exactly what happened. Get facts.

4. Staff meeting with students. Teachers are asked to review known facts and dispel rumors. Give only information needed. Staff members are encouraged to allow for the expression of grief in their classes in whatever way is appropriate for students. (All responses are acceptable, from severe reactions to no reactions at all. Be aware of students who are at risk during classroom discussion.) The guiding principle is to return to normal routine within each class as soon as possible. Whenever and wherever possible, teachers should discourage "glorification" of death. For example, if a student is heard to say, "I wouldn't have the guts to kill myself!" the teacher can respond, "Suicide is not a brave act! It is far more courageous to go on living and face your problems each day as you and I do." Help students separate reality from fantasy and de-mythologize the suicide act. Inform students of the availability of crisis team and counselors at school at any time during the school day. Inform them of community resources for mental health. It is helpful to distribute a written list of names, numbers, and addresses of resources. (The Grief Recovery Institute offers a national toll-free helpline Monday through Friday from 9:00 to 5:00 Pacific Standard Time at 1-800-445-4808.) Reassure students that any adult in the building is available to help in an emergency and is willing to listen. Members of the crisis team need to be consulted about any problems. Ask students to be supportive of one another and to escort any friend who is upset to a member of the crisis team or to the crisis center. Encourage students to discuss their feelings with their parents.

5. Announcement to be made by principal: "We regret to inform you of the

news that we have received. [Student's name], student in [grade] grade, has died. We will inform you about funeral arrangements when we receive them. At this time we want to extend our prayers and sympathy to the family and friends of [student's name].

6. Short crisis team meeting after school.

While it's important to assure teens that grief is normal, any emotion can be taken to dangerous extremes. And intense grief that isn't resolved within one year is not "good grief."[64]

Central Noble provided teachers with a list of symptoms of destructive grief with instructions to refer students who exhibit such symptoms to the counseling office. Christian psychologist Dr. Gary Collins lists several danger signs that we need to be aware of as we work with grieving teens. Among the most prevalent indications of pathological grief are the mourner's

- Increasing conviction that he or she is no longer valuable as a person
- Tendency to speak of the deceased in the present tense
- Subtle or open threats of self-destruction [see chapter 7 for warning signs of suicidal tendencies]
- Anti-social behavior
- Excessive hostility, moodiness, or guilt
- Excessive drinking or drug abuse
- Complete withdrawal and refusal to interact with others
- Impulsivity
- Persisting psychosomatic illnesses
- Veneration of objects that remind one of the deceased and link the mourner with the deceased
- Preoccupation with the dead person
- Refusal to change the deceased's room, or to dispose of his or her clothing and other possessions

- Extreme emotional expression
- Resistance to any offers of counseling or other help
- Stoic refusal to show emotion or to appear affected by the loss (this usually indicates denial and avoidance of grief)
- Intense busyness and unusual hyperactivity[65]

Collins suggests that people suffering "pathological grief" be led through " 're-grief': a re-experiencing of the grief process in order to free the counselee from his or her bondage to the deceased."[66] By going back to the time of death and working through the mourning process with teens, we can help them avoid some of the denial and avoidance mechanisms they have put in place to shield themselves from grief.

Marge felt that the district's plan worked well. "It was really rough, but I think we did the right thing by not canceling school. It's always better to grieve together.

"Now, a month later, I think we're on schedule with the mourning process. The students aren't afraid to talk about the deaths and still mention the three missing students' names. Probably five to 10 are still struggling with depression, not sleeping well, or visiting the graves frequently, but we have a regular, ongoing support group for them and any other students who need to talk about the deaths.

"One of the hardest adjustments was the 'empty seat.' It's always a strong reminder of the death. In fact, one student wouldn't go to class because he sat next to the empty seat. I think the teacher handled it well. She moved it to the back and said, 'This was Larry's seat. We're going to move it to the back and everyone else move up in the row.'"

Before I left Marge's office, I asked, "Would you do anything differently?"

"We held a memorial service, where a pastor spoke about the grief process, during first period Monday, after the accident on Friday night. We then gave the students the option of staying to talk with counselors and clergy spread throughout the auditorium or to go back to class. Probably 50 out of 600 stayed to talk and hug and cry.

"I think it would have been better to have everyone stay for 10 minutes. It didn't seem like there was time for closure.

"The tragedy brought people closer together and made them more responsive to each other," Marge said. "Barriers broke down between groups that didn't like each other. Now they were talking to each other and hugging one another."

ENDNOTES

1. J. C. Willke, *Abortion: Questions and Answers* (Cincinnati, Ohio: Hayes Publishing Co., Inc., 1985), 76.

2. *Statistical Abstract of the United States: The National Data Book* (Washington, D.C.: U.S. Department of Commerce, Economics, and Statistical Administration, 1998), No. 141.

3. Quoted by Kathy Koch, "School Violence," *Congressional Quarterly Researcher* (January–December 1998), 883.

4. Two interesting studies can be found in: Sharon Begley, "The Search for the Fountain of Youth," *Newsweek*, 5 March 1990, 44–48; and Staurt M. Berger, *Forever Young* (New York, New York: William Morrow and Company, Inc., 1989), 31–43.

5. Stuart M. Berger, *Forever Young* (New York, New York: William Morrow and Company, Inc., 1989), 19.

6. Berger, 19.

7. Michael R. Eades and Mary Dan Eades, *Protein Power* (New York, New York: Bantam Books, 1996).

8. Jeffery R. M. Kuntz, *The American Medical Association Family Medical Guide* (New York, New York: Random House, 1982), 16–17.

9. Quoted in the National Library of Medicine's MedLinePlus website at www.medlineplus.adam.com.

10. Bryce J. Christensen, "Critically Ill: The Family and Health Care in America," *Journal of the American Family Association* (June 1992): 12–13.

11. Christensen, 12–13.

12. Quoted by Christensen, 13.

13. Christensen, 12–13.

14. For more information about these stages, read Elisabeth Kübler-Ross, *On Death and Dying* (New York, New York: Macmillan, 1969).

15. Mary Fran Hazinki, *Nursing Care for the Critically Ill Child* (St. Louis, Missouri: Mosby Yearbooks, Inc., 1992), 42.

16. Elisabeth Kübler-Ross, *Questions and Answers on Death and Dying* (New York, New York: Macmillan, 1974), 3.

17. J. Kerby Anderson, *Life, Death & Beyond* (Grand Rapids, Michigan: Zondervan, 1980), 26.

18. James C. Dobson and Gary L. Bauer, *Children at Risk* (Dallas: Word, 1990), 147.

19. Dobson and Bauer, 146.

20. Daniel Callahan, *Setting Limits* (New York, New York: Simon & Shuster, 1987).

21. An excellent resource on the issues of abortion and euthanasia is Francis A. Schaeffer and C. Everett Koop, *Whatever Happened To The Human Race* (Old Tappan, New Jersey: Fleming H. Revell Co., 1979).

22. From UCLA Library's research site at www.library.ucla.edu/libraries/biomed/his/PaineExhibit/panel9.html.

23. Lee Sauer, "Former Satanist Proclaims He's a Christian," The News-Sun (3 March 1992): 1.

24. Quotes taken from interviews with students of Columbine High School.

25. "The Kids Are All Right," *Time* (16 August 1999): 77.

26. Koch, 884.

27. Koch, 883.

28. Koch, 884.

29. Koch, 885.

30. Koch 885,

31. This information was obtained from the U. S. Department of Education's "Guide to Safe Schools" website: www.ed.gov.

32. This information was obtained from the U. S. Department of Education's "Guide to Safe Schools" website: www.ed.gov.

33. Woodham quoted at www.abcnews.go.com/sections/us/DailyNews/pearl1108.html.

34. Julie Weiss, "Why the Young Kill," Newsweek (3 May 1999): 25.

35. Nancy Gibbs, "Special Report/ The Littleton Massacre," Time (3 May 1999).

36. This information was obtained from the U. S. Department of Education's "Guide to Safe Schools" website: www.ed.gov.

37. *Statistical Abstract of the United States*, No. 141.

38. An excellent resource is Melody Beattie's *A Reason to Live* (Wheaton, Illinois: Tyndale House Publishers, Inc., 1991).

39. Robert C. White and Leroy T. Gatman, "The Three Stages of Grief" in *Death & Dying: Opposing Viewpoints* (St. Paul, Minnesota: Greenhaven Press, 1980), 95–98.

40. Norm Wright, *Crisis Care: Hope for the Hurting* (Richardson, Texas: Grace Products Corporation, 1996), Tape 8.

41. John Irving, *A Prayer for Owen Meany* (New York, New York: Ballantine Books), 135.

42. C. S. Lewis, *A Grief Observed* (New York, New York: Bantam Books, 1961), 66–67.

43. Joyce Landorf, *Mourning Song* (Old Tappan, New Jersey: Fleming H. Revell Co., 1974), 18.

44. Concern for the Dying, 250 West 57th Street, New York, NY 10019. I would change the words "physical or mental disability" to read "an incurable terminal illness." "Physical disability" is far too vague. ("Dr. Death," Jack Kervorkian, has killed several of his patients who were *not* terminally ill.)

45. Scott Tuttle, Procurement Transplant Coordinator, Indiana Organ Procurement Organization, Inc., 719 Indiana Avenue, Indianapolis, IN 46202, (800) 356-7757.

46. Quoted in Anderson, *Life, Death & Beyond*, 89.

47. Anderson, 87.

48. Anderson, 73.

49. Shirley Maclaine, *Out on a Limb* (New York, New York: Bantam, 1983), 214.

50. MacLaine, 352.

51. MacLaine, 352.

52. Sylvia Cranston and Carey Williams, *Reincarnation: A New Horizon in Science, Religion, and Society* (New York, New York: Harmony, 1984), 23.

53. Quoted by Jess Stearn in *Intimates through Time: The Life Story of Edgar Cayce and His Companions through the Ages* (San Francisco, California: Harper & Row, 1989), 13.

54. Cranston and Williams, 7.

55. Stearn, 36.

56. Laurice Elehwany and Patricia Hermes, *My Girl* (New York, New York: Pocket Books, 1991), 106–107.

57. 12,000 "stadia" is about 1,400 miles or 2,200 kilometers; 144 cubits is about 200 feet or 65 meters.

58. "Loser of the Month" from *The Door* at http:// thedoormagazine.com.

59. John P. O'Connel, ed., *The Catholic Dictionary* (Chicago, Illinois: The Catholic Press, Inc., 1955), 196.

60. Max Lucado, *When Christ Comes* (Nashville, Tennessee: Word, 1999), 122.

61. C. S. Lewis, *The Great Divorce* (New York, New York: Macmillan, 1946), 66–67.

62. Elizabeth Richter, *Losing Someone You Love* (New York, New York: G. P. Putnam's Sons, 1986), 10.

63. Amy Hillyard Jensen, *Healing Grief* (Redmond, Washington: Medic Publishing Co., 1980), 15.

64. Part of the crisis plan at Central Noble High School, Albion, Ind., was drawn from the writings of J. Salanto.

65. Gary Collins, *Christian Counseling: A Comprehensive Guide* (Waco, Texas: Word Books, 1980), 418–419.

66. Collins, 420.